# Leadership
# 101

# DSC

# Leadership
# 101

## Margaret Lloyd &
## Brian Rothwell

Published by
Directory of Social Change
24 Stephenson Way
London NW1 2DP
Tel. 08450 77 77 07; Fax 020 7391 4804
E-mail: publications@dsc.org.uk
www.dsc.org.uk
from whom further copies and a full books catalogue are available.

Directory of Social Change is a Registered Charity no. 800517

First published 2007
Reprinted 2007

ISBN 978 1 903991 82 4

British Library Cataloguing in Publication Data

A catalogue record for this book is available from the British Library

Cover designed by Kate Bass
Illustration on page 143 by Ruth Murray
Page design and typesetting by Ben Cracknell Studios | Thomas Gravemaker
Printed and bound by Page Bros, Norwich

All Directory of Social Change departments in London:
08450 77 77 07

Directory of Social Change Northern Office:
Research 0151 708 0136

# Contents

# Foreword

We live in a world that is ever more demanding of leadership. Few organisations face a straightforward future free from strategic choices, resource constraints, and value judgements, based on a complex and never ending cascade of complex data from many sources. The business environment in any sector is a cocktail of risk in which good management and the ability to harness resources in the interests of the task in question is simply not enough. Organisations need leadership like never before.

The perennial question asked about leaders is – are they born or made? I think this book is intended to make people who are born and made to lead better leaders. The intelligent leader looks for any and all opportunities to build on their own, and learn from the experiences of others in order to enhance their potency in the many and varied situations leadership demands of them. They need the ability to synthesize logic, emotion and values to make decisions and analyse situations. This is a difficult concept to apply in reality.

Finally, it is my view that one of the core requirements of leaders is to recognise and encourage other leaders. It is the mark of the truly mature leader that he/she is surrounded by leaders. In fact, leadership is what happens when the "leader isn't in the room". It is the mark of a leadership culture in which hierarchy is replaced with the opportunity to lead within the context of the situation in which an individual finds themselves. This kind of leadership will be the mark of the successful organisation in the future. In my view, it is the only way of leading in complex and challenging times.

This book contains practical steps that leaders can take on the never ending journey to truly inspired and inspiring leadership. I recommend it to you in the hope it provides ideas and stimulation in the difficult, rewarding and necessary task of leadership.

Lord Victor Adebowale CBE
Chief Executive
Turning Point

# About the authors

**Margaret Lloyd**

After graduating with a degree in astrophysics in 1974, Margaret spent a long career in public service, initially in teaching and then in various senior roles in the Inland Revenue. She is now a performance coach and leadership consultant with a particular interest in organisational development. She is a founder-director, with Sheridan Maguire, of Walking With Leaders Ltd, a consultancy specialising in improving business results through developing effective leaders/coaches and releasing creativity at work.

She works across sectors including central and local government, education, media, the police and charitable and voluntary organisations in the UK and Europe. She has designed and run group workshops, senior strategy meetings, conferences and symposia, facilitated training days and lectured extensively to large and small groups and she coaches and mentors directors and CEOs on a one-to-one basis. Margaret has also written on organisational transformation for the *Journal of Change Management*.

Margaret is a professional business coach certificated by the University of Strathclyde and an accredited MBTI (Myers Briggs Type Indicator) practitioner. She is also an associate consultant and programme leader for The Campaign for Leadership, a Fellow of the Institute of Quality Assurance and Chair of Trustees of the Directory of Social Change.

Married with two young adult children, Margaret lives with her husband in Berkshire and is a compulsive plantswoman.

**Brian Rothwell**

After graduating in economics from LSE in 1970, Brian spent two and a half decades employed by top ranking plcs in the insurance industry, 15 years with Royal Insurance and ten years with Sedgwick. He has held board positions with responsibility for sales and marketing as well as personnel and training. He is a fellow and a practitioner of the Chartered Insurance Institute.

In 1996 Brian undertook the development of his own portfolio career. He is currently a freelance coach, lecturer and writer.

During the last 10 years Brian has worked with more than 70 organisations. He has worked in the UK, Europe, North America and Russia. He has been a keynote leadership speaker on more than 100 conferences since 1996.

He has co-authored *The X & Y of Leadership*, a book that explores the leadership implications of gender.

In his spare time he is a qualified athletics coach who enjoys orienteering. He lives in Hampshire and is married with two adult children.

# Introduction

All leaders have notions for making the future better than the present. Somewhere among those ideas, plans and potential targets there are some tremendous things waiting to happen. The equivalent of the heart bypass operation or the mobile telephone is just around the corner, about to be thought up. But – and it is a big but – thinking time is nowadays a very rare entry in any busy executive's diary.

Leadership has been called the most researched and misunderstood topic on earth, so why should we bother to add to the fuss? For us leadership is about creating bottom line success with a real 'feel good' factor – where everyone achieves more, is more successful, more valued and happier than they were before. As busy executives we longed for a plain English digest of the latest theories with an explanation of how to put them into practice, when they would be helpful and what the pitfalls might be, and for someone to tell us honestly how to do the hard bits without making things worse.

*Here is Edward Bear, coming downstairs now, bump, bump, bump on the back of his head behind Christopher Robin. It is, as far as he knows, the only way of coming downstairs, but sometimes he feels that there really is another way, if only he could stop bumping and think of it.*

A.A. Milne,
*Winnie-the-Pooh*

Eventually we have written it ourselves. This book is a summary of all the useful things we have found over the years that have actually helped us to get the job done well in an enthusiastic and relatively harmonious way.

One successful managing director once told us that he wished to maintain the mystique of good leadership, implying that the keys to success should not be easily available to all. His view was that he had to learn his leadership skills and attributes the hard way, by making mistakes, and that all potential leaders needed to do the same. We disagree. We believe that we need leaders to be as successful as possible, as often as possible, so everyone can share in that success. We see no reason why leaders should have to learn by making avoidable mistakes through lack of information.

This is a working handbook on leadership that busy people can refer to often and particularly in times of difficulty and uncertainty. We provide explanations of the tools and techniques that will enable ordinary people to lead and to lead well. We believe that our messages apply equally to leaders of a multi-national company, a private business, part of the public sector, a charity or a non-governmental organisation.

Our objective is to simplify and demystify rather than to complicate and make mysterious. We have tried to write in simple straightforward language that everyone from the office junior to the chair of the board can relate to and understand, and to avoid the jargon that both confuses and annoys. We have included all the lessons that we have learned from our own careers as well as the best of the current leading-edge academic and practical thinking on the subject.

## How to use this book

The first chapter brings together all the current leadership theories and definitions, explains how they arose and the essential thinking involved. In a series of questions and answers we attempt to deal with the commonest concerns about leadership that we hear from people at work and so set the scene for taking action.

Chapter 2 outlines the five circles of influence, key areas that will demand your leadership attention sooner or later. We suggest that you take some time to think about these in terms of your own organisation, decide which get most of your attention and which least, and whether you have the balance right.

The rest of the book contains 101 leadership tips, ranging from how to think like a leader through to how to deal with the witchcraft that emanates from head office. Each of these is primarily related to one of the five circles so we have arranged this part of the book in five steps to make finding things easier and to enable you to start wherever you are most interested right now. There is no 'right' place to start, just follow your own interests.

Each tip is cross-referenced to linked topics covered elsewhere and to suggested further reading for those who are interested in learning more. If the books we recommend are out of print we suggest you conduct an Internet search on www.abe.com or www.bookfinder.com. When we checked, they were all there.

### Step 1: thinking like a leader

How to use the leadership theories in Chapter 1, what to do and how to avoid the possible pitfalls.

### Step 2: creating a vision

This explains what a vision is, why you might want to bother, how to go about it and how to use the vision once you have finally decided on it.

### Step 3: choosing a set of values

Values are like the operating system of a PC, usually hidden behind all that is on the desktop, quietly enabling things to happen in an expected way. However, put two PCs with different operating systems together and expect them to communicate – you will have problems. So it is with people and with organisations. If the values don't match, or are not understood, leaders will have problems. This section explains how to choose your values, use them and share them appropriately.

### Step 4: recognising that people are different

We all know that people are different yet sometimes we forget to think about this when we are in a hurry to get things done. This section explains a simple way to recognise the main characteristics of different thinking styles, how to recognise them in those you meet and how to adapt your own leadership approach so that you maximise your effectiveness with everyone.

### Step 5: achieving extraordinary results

This is the largest section of the book and contains practical tips on how to deal with the common problems of leading an organisation, managing everything and still finding time to think and to have a life outside work.

A friend to whom we e-mailed a pre-publication version of the book tells us that he keeps it on his desktop and looks at a tip a day. That way he either learns something, finds out what he already knows or marshals his arguments to send to us, generating an interesting conversation. Another told us that she keeps the embryo version of the book on her desk and refers to it whenever she has a leadership problem.

However you decide to use it, we believe that you will find much here that is familiar; there is no rocket science in this book. We expect that you will disagree with some of it and we hope that you will find some useful insights that help you to expand your leadership influence.

This is not a book to be read in one sitting. We hope that you will write your own insights in the margins, mark the relevant pages and make it your own working document.

As Mr Spock might have said,

'Lead well and prosper'.

# Acknowledgements

To the many people who have helped and supported us both in our work and in the writing of this book – thank you! In particular, we would like to single out the following and thank them for their advice, guidance, inspiration, interest, time and leadership expertise.

Lord Victor Adebowale CBE
Debra Allcock Tyler
Andrew Campbell-Hart
Julia Cleverdon
Chris Day
Dr John Edmonson
John Garnett
Lance Garrard
Jim Graves
John Green
John Horrocks
Richard Livesey-Haworth
Chris Lloyd
Sheridan Maguire
John Martin
Lucy Muir-Smith
Ray Noyes

Richard Olivier
Steve O'Smotherley
Ann Paul
Josie Payne
Geraldine Peacock
Norman Rothwell
Sue Rothwell
Bill Taylor
Liz Taylor
Ben Thompson-McCausland
Anne Stratton
Lisa van der Wekken
John Walkley
Miki Walleczek
Sir Peter White
Steve Williams

# Chapter **1**
# Setting the scene

## What is leadership?

Leadership is all about people. It is about nothing else but people. People are the first note on the keyboard of leadership that has to be hit and the last. And every note in between must be hit perfectly for them to perform consistently above their own expectations.

The tricks to becoming a good leader are to be able to recognise what is wrong and how to put it right, to elicit the cooperation of followers, to listen to the constantly changing needs of others both inside and outside your own operation, and to put the needs of the organisation ahead of your own.

Leadership is that simple and … that difficult.

Most people at work do not think of their managers as leaders. On the one hand their manager could be 'a nice guy but a bit weak' or on the other they could be 'incredibly intelligent, very successful but she eats people so I wouldn't work for her'.

Successful leaders are comparatively rare. They embody the personal qualities and values that make people like them and are also successful, which makes people respect them. Liking and respect are the twin factors that will cause followers to go the extra mile willingly.

## Is leadership different from management?

Business class travellers now carry slim books on leadership whereas in the 1990s they carried thick tomes on management. Management is now a dirty word – it reeks of taking away people's livelihoods using excuses like 'de-layering' and 'right sizing'.

The jargon-filled pronouncements of organisations in the 1990s are now deemed bad memories of a bygone age. Organisational aims such as 'We intend to become the best managed organisation in the public sector' were accompanied by huge spending on consultants to achieve the objective. The promotion of cold management efficiency was then at its height.

In contrast, today large organisations have kicked out the consultants and leadership has a warm human ring to it suggesting accessibility, collective effort and teamwork. Whilst no one states that management techniques are unimportant, managers today are deemed invisible deskbound cowards hiding behind their computer screens. Leaders are visible heroes walking the job and setting the example.

*Leadership is of the spirit, compounded of personality and vision; its practice is an art. Management is of the mind, more a matter of the accurate calculation of timetables, methods and statistics. Its practice is a science.*

William Slim,
Field Marshal

We think that view is too extreme. We do, however, believe that there is a fundamental distinction between management and leadership and that both are absolutely essential for an organisation to succeed.

Management is primarily about non-human resources or things, whilst leadership is about people. Management is a science taught as a university degree subject whereas leadership can be termed the art of possibility. All leaders want to change the status quo. If no change is needed a manager will make sure that things are done well. However if change is needed, call for a leader.

Management involves using the left hemisphere of the brain to devise logical processes, project plans, performance indicators and risk registers. The right hemisphere is needed for effective leadership, to see the patterns of activity in the sector, imagine how things might be different and spark an idea in the team. A manager uses the left-hand side of his brain to build his budget; a leader uses the right-hand side of her brain to inspire her staff to achieve the budget. In order to persuade and influence others we need to be able to visualise a future that does not currently exist, to think up creative solutions to problems and to be able to sense when others are struggling or feeling low. And to take effective action we need good management.

## The leadership management matrix

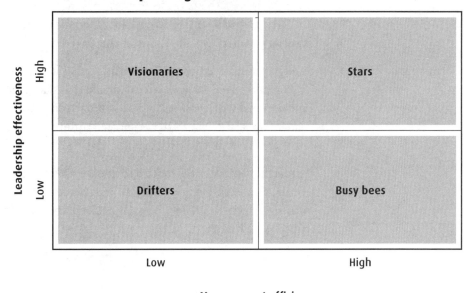

Source: Manfred Kets de Vries, *The leadership mystique*

19

Leaders can only achieve what their followers want them to achieve. Managers can sack staff who disagree with them and so shut up the rest for a time. However, successful leadership is dependent on the wishes of the constituents. Leaders can only achieve what they persuade their followers to want to achieve. If the leader tells the right story, tells the story in the right way, nominates a purpose in tune with those of the followers and gets the timing of the story right, he or she will succeed.

Margaret Thatcher was ousted from the prime ministerial chair in 1990 because she failed to absorb the public mood about the poll tax. She was in a position where she was telling the wrong story at the wrong time. She was out of tune with her constituents. In spite of her notable successes in the past, her constituents (in this case her fellow Conservative MPs) rejected her as a leader.

## Is leadership temporary?

Leadership is a transient and temporary condition. It floats around and moves like the magnetic North Pole. A leader only gets so many chances to succeed before followers look somewhere else for a new leader.

Leadership is to do with engaging the emotions of others. This emotional attachment of followers cannot be commanded. Managers can manage until they retire but leaders can only lead as long as they can get people to go along with them. If a leader destroys the trust of a follower, that follower may well remain at work for economic or security reasons, but will not be led, they will submit to a managed relationship only.

A management relationship can be perfectly satisfactory if it is brisk and businesslike with cool attention paid to tasks and results. It can be unemotional with a job-orientated approach on both sides. In contrast, a leadership relationship will not succeed through coolness. There must be emotion, warmth, enthusiasm and a stirring of the blood.

Leadership is temporary for two reasons. Firstly, the situation that requires leadership may come to an end. Leadership is about helping teams reach goals. When the goal is reached, there may be no further need for leadership.

Winston Churchill led the United Kingdom successfully through the Second World War, but the electorate rejected him in the 1945 election.

Secondly, today's respected leader may be out of touch with the reality of tomorrow. The goals that once called forth all of the leader's skills and attributes may have changed. Tomorrow's struggle may, in fact, be diametrically opposed to everything that a leader stood for yesterday.

Mikhail Gorbachev led the transformation of the Soviet Union and that led to the dismantling of the Berlin Wall. However, once into the brave new world he had envisioned, his constituents, the Russian people, rejected him.

A good leader must recognise that there is a time to lead and a time to manage – a time to lead and a time to follow.

## Is leadership a good thing?

The concept of leadership embraces Churchill, who roused the British nation to go to war when perhaps a majority of the population did not want to fight. Most would agree that he changed the world of his time for the better. It also embraces Jim Jones, the founder of the People's Temple cult in Guyana. In 1974 Jones led 914 of his followers in an act of mass suicide. Influenced by his leadership, followers fed cyanide to 240 of their own children. Most would agree that he changed the world of his time for the worse.

*What these experiments told us was that there is something bizarre about all human beings, not just Germans and Russians.*

Keith Grint, Reader in organisational behaviour, Oxford Saïd Business School

Famous people with memorable leadership gifts include Nelson Mandela, Mahatma Ghandi and Abraham Lincoln. They embody our highest sense of what it means to be human. However it is irrefutable that others who persuaded their followers to indulge in mass murder, such as Adolf Hitler, Saddam Hussein and Joseph Stalin, also possessed considerable leadership attributes. They serve to warn us how low leaders can cause their followers to sink.

After the horrors of the gas chambers and the mass burial pits orchestrated by Hitler and Stalin in the Second World War became common knowledge, leadership was viewed as dangerous. Two chilling psychological experiments in the United States provided devastating evidence of the dangers involved.

In the Milgram experiment, volunteers were engaged to ask questions of a man strapped to a chair with an electrode attached to his arm. If the man got the answer wrong, the volunteer was instructed to administer increasingly powerful electric shocks. It was a trick – the man in the chair was an actor who screamed as though he had been shocked, but there was no electric charge. In spite of mounting screams of pain, 65% of the volunteers were persuaded to punish their prisoners up to the maximum – a lethal charge of 450 volts.

In the Asch experiment, three people were shown lines on a screen. Together they had to select the longest line – the correct choice was always obvious. Only one of the group of three was the experiment subject – the other two were experimenters. After a few rounds the two experimenters began to choose the wrong lines. At first the subjects were confused, but then, almost always, they would go along with the patently wrong opinions of the other two people present.

The results of both experiments are still widely seen as conclusive. Most people can easily be pressurised, or led, into conducting acts of unbelievable cruelty or into denying what they have seen with their own eyes.

Such startling evidence of the nakedness of the power of leaders can inspire a suspicion, even a hatred, of leadership. This was a prevailing view in the Western world in the late 1950s and the 1960s. A powerful popular mindset existed that there should be no leaders at all.

*People must take part in all of the decisions that affect their lives.*
Ben Brewster, student activist, London School of Economics, 1966

Coupled with the anti-authoritarian messages of the Campaign for Nuclear Disarmament, the protests against the Vietnam War and the marches organised by the anti-apartheid movement, a view existed that leadership was untrustworthy. This prevailing opinion helped to develop the power of the trade unions under which managers were denied the right to influence the workforce without the permission of shop stewards and convenors.

At the level of the large organisation with thousands of employees, or a nation, this view of the organisation as a commune was, and still is, patently unviable. Someone has to choose between opposing opinions, views and potential courses of action. We need someone to make the difficult decisions and we need to hold them accountable for so doing. The buck has to stop somewhere.

Since the destruction of the World Trade Centre on 11 September 2001 leadership has become a much more urgent issue for the world at large. Giuliani and Blair, Bush and Rumsfeld, as well as Bin Laden and Saddam Hussein have all strutted their leadership stuff on the world stage. Suddenly we seem to have woken up to the simple fact that leaders can either be a force for good or a force for evil.

According to a survey by Roffey Park, the business education specialists, published in 2005, mistrust of leaders is spreading rapidly from politics to business. This survey discovered that one in four managers say they have lost trust in their company leaders. They cite corporate excess, bullying, harassment, stress, internal politicking, the fat-cat pay issue and corporate scandals among the causes. Almost half thought the fallout from the Enron affair was 'increased cynicism and distrust'. The 600 managers who took part in this survey did not value the leaders they were paid to follow.

There is no neutral zone in leadership. Followers categorise their leaders as either 'good' or 'bad'.

## Do leaders perform a valued role?

When leaders get it right, they perform a valued role in our society. They always have done and they always will do. They produce extraordinary results.

In the early 1970s, two ordinary Irish housewives, Betty Williams, a Protestant, and Mairead Corrigan, a Catholic, formed an organisation called Peace People. Their aim was to start a movement to overcome the hatred that was marring the lives of all people in their country. This aligned with the aims and beliefs of the majority. In 1976 the two women were awarded the Nobel Peace Prize.

Leaders are the dreamers who can see the possibility of how things could be different and tomorrow better than today, and who have the courage to set about making that happen. Without leaders we would become increasingly hide-bound and begin to stagnate. We need leaders to give us a sense of identity, purpose and direction and to make possible the ideas that might otherwise have remained wishes. Change is inevitable, leaders help us to see the positives and solve the problems that we alone cannot solve. However enthusiastic, unless leader and followers share the same vision, values and beliefs leaders can and do fail.

We need leaders who can give our lives a purpose, a reason for living, a direction, and who make us feel better about ourselves every time we meet them.

## Do we need leaders?

There are some who would argue that we don't need leaders at all; we simply need people who listen. One American marine commander in the Second World War made a point of asking his troops where he went wrong after every enemy contact and what he could have done better. He won countless engagements but was sidelined by his superiors, who hated and feared his methods.

When Boeing built their first 747 jumbo jet, they found that it was 50 tons too heavy. They asked the workforce how to reduce the weight and the problem was solved. Jack Welch of General Electric, probably the most successful, and certainly the most admired industrial leader of recent years, spent most of his time just listening and talking to people. Leading sports coaches like Sven-Goran Erikson, the former manager of the England football team, and Duncan Fletcher, the coach of the England cricket team, are renowned for listening to their players.

*Leaders are deep listeners who abandon their ego to the talents of others.*

Warren Bennis, leadership professor

However, leaders do more than just listen. They envisage, inspire, support and make tough decisions. They are passionate about what their organisation can achieve. They let their followers know that they have a great belief in their potential to achieve the extraordinary.

Sometimes leaders deliberately don't listen. Margaret Thatcher made a point of not listening to the consensus builders, the 'wets' in her cabinet, and yet went on to win the Falklands war and to tame the destructive powers of the trade unions.

And there are others who argue that leadership is dangerous and they quote leaders who have employed others to undertake devious, unjust and sometimes downright illegal means to achieve their ends. They can quote many examples – Robert Maxwell, Boesky and Levine (who manipulated the junk savings bond scam in the USA in the 1990s) and the executive directors of Enron. And in this sense the doubters about leadership are right.

Our position is that we need leaders who have openly declared values that are in agreement with the values of those they lead and whose actions demonstrate this. Our advice to followers is to ensure that the leader lives by a set of values that all followers can buy into, that the organisation's values are known and agreed and that they, the followers, are in complete agreement with the vision that the leader sets out to achieve.

## Do leaders need to be in top positions?

It is a common misconception that leaders are only found at the top of their organisations. Some leaders *are* at the top of their organisations, although the skills and behaviours of leadership can be exercised at any level. Wherever we are in an organisation, most of us are almost simultaneously leaders, subordinates and colleagues.

The knowledge and skills necessary to make organisations work are decentralised. The board may have spent hours poring over the latest market analysis when drawing up the new three-year plan and the office junior knows how many of the latest batch of marketing materials have been returned by the post office – so true power is decentralised and leadership is needed at all levels in an organisation.

Many individuals who are followers at work are leaders in their leisure time – perhaps organising the annual jumble sale, coaching the junior football team or running the neighbourhood watch scheme. All three of these tasks require leadership skills and attributes for a successful outcome. The successful senior managers in large companies like ICI, ICL and Vodafone use these same skills and attributes.

Leadership has been demonstrated by thousands of women and men throughout the history of business, politics, sport and warfare. It is, however, only espoused by the media and given publicity when there are big issues, serious crises or great forces at work. In normal times leadership is just part of the invisible backdrop of daily life. It goes on without attention.

## Can anyone be a leader?

It is tempting to answer with a resounding 'No' because some people at work choose to be constantly cynical, defensive of the status quo, object to any new idea and generally obstruct progress. Yet in extreme situations, for example where life is threatened, most people prove themselves capable of being extraordinary. So we believe that we can all improve our leadership capabilities if we are prepared to try and to put some thought and effort into it.

> *Most people can improve their leadership capabilities with a little thought and practice.*
>
> William Slim,
> Field Marshal

Napoleon Bonaparte believed that there was a marshal's baton in every soldier's knapsack. Given the right time and circumstances he thought that every soldier in his army had the potential to be a general and lead the army in his absence. This may not be true. There can be a difference between the attributes needed to lead in an emergency and those required to keep going day after day.

For emergency leadership a large dose of adrenalin, coupled with a threat to a core value (we must help one another) is enough to galvanise action, and the need for action is much more important than how the instructions are phrased. There is no need to think about the wider context – sharp focus on the here and now is what is required.

For day-to-day continuous leadership, in addition to sufficient intelligence to grasp the big picture, a leader needs an abundance of emotional intelligence – the ability to manage relationships and motivate others. Not everyone possesses this. It can be developed but there are people who simply do not attain a sufficient degree of self-awareness and awareness of the motivations of others to become good leaders.

The art of relationships is, in large part, a skill in influencing the emotions of others. These are the abilities that underpin successful leadership. Good leaders need a high level of emotional intelligence. Good leaders are aware of the effect that their words and actions have on other people.

## Why should I want to become a leader?

Given the current media determination to expose all the failings, usually sexual or financial, of those who choose to accept a public leadership position, a serious current question has emerged – 'Who are the people who can be trusted to lead?'. This media pressure has also posed what we think is a more serious question – 'Why should sane, thinking individuals choose to pick up the leadership mantle?'.

Leadership can involve considerable personal sacrifice. The responsibilities can be huge and they often involve operating in unforeseen circumstances. Leaders have to make bigger decisions than those around them – particularly where people are concerned. Sometimes the very big decisions have to be made alone and can only be resolved after the most profound, painful and inescapable soul-searching. Often the reasons cannot be explained for years afterwards so the leader has to live with unfair or ill-informed criticism.

Only a leader can realise what it feels like when the buck finally does stop. She or he may have heard this phrase time and again without realising the extent of that hollow feeling of isolation and exposure that occurs when there is no one else left to receive the buck or even to offer advice.

Leaders often have doubts of their own abilities to deal with such situations. In private moments an acute sense of personal inadequacy may overwhelm us. Shakespeare, in *Henry V*, calls this 'the dark night of the soul'.

As society widens the leadership brief to include social responsibility, ethics, sustainability and responsible corporate governance, it is putting an even greater burden on the shoulders of leaders in organisations.

The cost of leadership can also include a shortage of personal and family time, giving up hobbies, an intrusion of work at unsocial hours, intensive travel and a surfeit of e-mail that has to be read and answered. A current executive director of BT reported to us that he found journalists searching his dustbin for evidence of anything that could make him unsuitable for his leading role in the company.

Consequently, many individuals are now choosing not to accept the leadership load. One in ten Londoners is now a 'free worker'. They have chosen to work as freelancers, reporting to no one but themselves and responsible for no one but themselves.

However, leaders continually step forward into leadership roles because they care. They want to right a wrong, they want to change things for the better and they want to make the future an improvement on today.

## What can we learn from history?

As we examine the present and attempt to look into the future we tend to concentrate only on the dramatic and current changes taking place here and now. It is a commonly quoted, but questionable, fact that we live in the era of the maximum amount of change in history. Perhaps the Victorian generations lived through more change than we have done. They did after all move *en masse* from an agricultural society to an industrial economy and in doing so moved from the countryside into the towns. Perhaps those who lived through two world wars in the twentieth century experienced more profound convulsions than we are doing today.

However we do know that globalisation, changing customer expectations, competitor initiatives and the ease of access to information make corporate investment decisions an extremely chancy business. And we know that at an individual level careers have moved from cradle-to-grave security to become journeys into 'the land of I don't knows' in a generation.

Faced with these increasing complexities, it is all too easy to ignore, or discount, what effective leaders have been doing for centuries throughout the history of industry, trade and commerce. Similarly in government, the armed forces, public service, religion, teaching, science and medicine, competent leadership has always been the prime mover for progress.

Current leadership role models such as Richard Branson and Anita Roddick have much more 'street credibility' with students of the subject than Queen Elizabeth I and Alexander the Great. Much of our learning, particularly from role models, is essentially an imitative process and it is understandable that the current icons are a more appropriate source of inspiration than remote and distant examples of the leadership art.

Sun-Tzu wrote his treatise on leadership called *The art of war* 2,500 years ago. He nominates seven aspects of leadership that are likely to be quickly assessed by followers.

1 Competence and readiness to keep learning open.
2 Sense of purpose and commitment to goals.
3 Self-discipline and self-respect.
4 Achievement and accomplishments.
5 Sense of accountability and responsibility.
6 Ability to build effective relationships.
7 Readiness to lead by example.

If we compare this 2,500-year-old thesis with the findings of modern leadership research projects, the results are remarkably similar. Kouzes and Posner identify 13 behaviours and actions that currently constitute personal power and perceived credibility among leaders.

They are:

1 Challenging the process, not accepting the status quo.
2 Searching for opportunities.

*Never let the future disturb you. You will meet it with the same weapons of reason which arm you against the present.*

Marcus Aurelius, Roman general

3   Experimenting and trying new ideas and options.

4   Inspiring shared visions.

5   Envisioning a future for the business and its marketplace.

6   Enlisting others through networking and dialogue.

7   Enabling others to act, facilitating effective performance.

8   Strengthening others and building on these strengths.

9   Fostering collaboration, through alliances and coalitions.

10  Modelling the way and path-finding.

11  Setting an example which may involve some sacrifice.

12  Celebrating accomplishments.

13  Recognising people's contributions.

If we accept that Sun-Tzu was writing about leadership in the context of war, whereas Kouzes and Posner were concerned with business success, and allow a little leeway for development of language, this comparison confirms the timelessness of sound effective leadership and the principles and practices that continue to be at the heart of leading others to success.

The past is there to be learned from – not lived in. It is vital that we do not throw the baby out with the bathwater. There is gold to be found in the examination of the behaviours of the leaders of yesterday. We ignore the lessons they can teach us at our peril in our rush to embrace the latest leadership fads, fashions and fetishes.

The Hegelian dialectic of taking the best of the past – the thesis – then combining it with the best of new thinking – the antithesis – and merging them appropriately – into the synthesis – remains as relevant today as the day Hegel wrote it in 1807.

Hegel's is a concept that does not make the past bad, wrong or irrelevant. He acknowledges the strength of both old and new thinking. His is a philosophy of 'win-win' plus 'both-and' solutions and it is superior to the 'either-or' answers to leadership problems espoused by so many recent authors.

The history of human civilisation provides a very rich source of leadership object lessons and success stories as well as many examples of incompetence, crass mistakes and gross immorality when there has been a cynical abuse of the leadership role. We can squander our leadership heritage by ignoring or rejecting the ample and relevant lessons of experience.

## Leadership today

Leadership is constantly referred to in the newspapers and reported on in the media. The success of Clive Woodward in building the English rugby union team into world champions has introduced the leadership debate into sport. And there is interest in learning from leadership success in sport and translating the messages into business. Sir Clive Woodward claims that his success in sport came about because he transferred business leadership techniques into rugby.

Although it has been a topic of interest to historians and philosophers since ancient times, it was only around the 1950s that serious scientific studies of the psychology of leadership began. In these last 50 years scholars and writers have offered us in excess of 350 definitions of the term. During the 1990s 10 academic papers a day were published on the subject.

There are currently more than 40 institutions in Britain running regular open courses on the subject. They include business schools, universities, charities and commercial companies. There is even a Centre for Leadership in Schools. They embrace domains from the academic to the physically testing and everything in between. Countless books on leadership are published every year and in every organisation of repute, the training department has an offering on leadership for its managers and staff.

There are as many different approaches to the subject as there are authors and researchers, a fact that can be very confusing to the student and frustrating to the busy leader who wants to find out more about her chosen field of endeavour.

## The main theories

*Leadership is the most heavily researched and most misunderstood phenomenon on earth.*

Michael Williams, author

The theories all fall into one or more of the following six broad categories that are more or less chronological in order of their development.

1   The qualities or traits approach – what does a leader have to be?

2   The knowledge-based approach – what does a leader have to know?

3   Functional, behavioural or action-centred approach – what does a leader have to do?

4   Dyadic or relationship-based approach, which distinguishes between the relationship of the leader with followers both as individuals and as a team.

5 Contingency or situational approach which concludes that successful leadership depends on the prevailing situation.

6 Constitutive approach, which states that a leader's role is to turn visionary ideas into a story that followers can relate to, make sense of and understand.

None of these approaches is sufficient on its own to ensure that the leadership basket of attributes and skills is full. To be effective, we need to understand all of them and to practise using them to be able to apply them appropriately at work.

We contend that leadership involves a mix of inborn personal traits, day-to-day behaviours and relationships with followers, and that is dependent on the situation prevailing. In a leadership sense there must be an appropriate fit between the leader's behaviour, the situation in which the leader is operating and the followers involved. Or, in other words, leadership never happens in isolation.

To understand leadership we need to examine not only the personal make up of the leader, their character type, values, attitudes, beliefs, position, experience and behaviours, but also the make up of the followers. Plus we should look at the specifics of the particular situation a leader finds themselves in (as our publisher put it, 'identifying the shit you are sitting in'), the nature of the task, what is good and bad about the organisation, the corporate culture, the nature of the industry and the socio-economic and political environment.

Above all, leaders need to recognise that people are different. One leadership approach will not work for all individuals. Leaders need a range of approaches to motivate different people to produce results.

## Qualities

The qualities or traits approach is the oldest and this argues that leaders are born with the necessary personal leadership qualities rather than made. It is part of the eternal nature versus nurture debate. To us it seems evident that personal traits such as courage, self-confidence, intelligence and a willingness to take risks are part of the personality that makes a successful leader.

### Knowledge-based

This second approach is derived from the dictum that he, or she, who knows the most about the situation in hand is the best individual to lead. We think it is logical that leaders need to know enough about the task in hand to be able to make credible decisions that will both satisfy followers and improve performance. However we do not agree with the view that the person who knows the most will always make the best leader.

### Functional

It also seems logical to us to conclude that successful leaders display the personal traits they possess through their behaviour. Consequently many researchers have examined the behaviour of leaders to determine what behaviours comprise a successful leadership style and how particular behaviours relate to effective leadership.

Dr John Adair epitomised this approach with his memorable, interlocking three-circle model 'action-centred leadership' which stated that a leader had to achieve the task, build the team and develop individuals.

### Dyadic

Leaders, of course, need others to follow. Later research distinguished behaviours occurring between a leader and each individual follower, differentiating between one-on-one behaviour and leader-to-group behaviour. In other words, leadership is dependent upon the relationship forged between the leader and individual followers and the leader and followers as a team.

Concentrate on the relationship for the sake of the relationship was a theme expressed. From trusting relationships can come business possibilities, opportunities and actions and then, hopefully, great results.

### Contingency

Contingent means 'dependent on something else'.

This theory states that it all depends on what is happening at the time. The failure to find universal leader traits or behaviours that would always determine success led researchers in another direction. Whilst leader behaviour was still examined, the central focus of this approach was the situation in which the leadership occurred.

The basic tenet was that behaviour effective in some situations might be ineffective under different conditions. Thus the effectiveness of leader behaviour is contingent upon organisational situations. Leaders therefore need to develop a repertoire of skills for use according to the situation.

## Constitutive

This theory comes from metaphysics and fuzzy logic studies into the way the universe is formed and how its components link together. Constitutive means 'having the power to establish something'. It means forming parts of something into a whole.

Complex organisations in a fast-changing world need leaders who can hold and communicate the core purpose and meaning of the work.

Constitutive theory brings the concept of vision into leadership. In it the leader's role is to turn visionary ideas into a story that those involved can relate to, make sense of and understand. It is the job of the leader to paint a picture of the future that is better than the present or the past. It is the leader's job to inspire the hope that tomorrow can be better than today. However, leaders can only do this if the story is aligned to the beliefs and values of the followers, and meets their aspirations.

## Where are we now?

Leadership today involves a full understanding of all six approaches outlined above and a willingness to think about the organisation as a system that can adapt positively to change if we lead it well.

Today the leader needs to be a good storyteller to create the strong sense of 'organisational self' by creating and communicating a clear vision and a shared understanding of guiding principles.

And, just as importantly, the leader must embody the story in her or his own life. The leader must walk the talk. He or she must act as though the vision is already in existence. And that vision must be greater than the individual. 'A land of milk and honey' inspired the Israelites in the desert when 'follow me I'm Moses and God has talked to me' might have been less effective. Being in the service of something greater than personal ambition is a powerful message to others provided they share the same vision, values and beliefs.

*Nature is always hinting at us. It hints over and over again. And suddenly we take the hint.*

Robert Frost, author

33

When a leader is talking to experts the story must be sophisticated in order to be credible. However, when a leader is talking to a mixed group, the story must be sufficiently elemental to be understood by the most unsophisticated person present.

Martin Luther King delivered perhaps the greatest leadership speech of the twentieth century to 250,000 people at the Lincoln Memorial in 1963:

> I have a dream that one day on the red hills of Georgia, the sons of former slaves and the sons of former slave owners will be able to sit down together at the table of brotherhood.

> I have a dream that one day even the state of Mississippi, sweltering in the heat of injustice and oppression, will be transformed into an oasis of freedom and justice.

> I have a dream that my four little children will one day live in a nation where they will not be judged by the colour of their skin but by the content of their character.

> I have a dream today.

The message was superbly elemental. In only 108 words he touched the emotions of his audience.

The greatest speech of the nineteenth century was perhaps that given by Abraham Lincoln at the burial ground for the Union dead at Gettysburg in 1863. He took just 272 words to express the view that 'Government of the people, by the people, for the people shall not perish from the earth'.

Both speeches illustrate the importance of vision and values in linking the purpose of the leader to that of the followers. This can only be done effectively when the aims, values and beliefs of the leader align with the aims and values of the followers, the constituents. The leadership message must be connected to deeply held beliefs and make sense of the work needed in the context of them – leaders are the modern troubadours. The message must also give rise to a sense of identity among the followers – it must give meaning and purpose to their roles as well as to what needs to be done.

## Organisations today

In today's environment of flat management structures, increased customer expectations, just-in-time supply processes, investment uncertainty and the withdrawal of government from social support, organisations are increasingly complex and leaders need to be flexible and to think on their feet. What worked yesterday is not going to work as well tomorrow. Traditional hierarchies, derived from the model of the organisation as a machine, are now recognised as too rigid and unable to create effective communication and feedback quickly enough in a fast-changing environment.

The latest thinking is that organisations can be better understood using the biological model of complex adaptive systems. Complexity theory is a mathematical tool used to investigate systems such as living organisms, the weather or evolution, which contain a large network of independent components all interacting in complex ways. We now know that it is the interaction of these components, the sharing of knowledge between them, which controls the structure and behaviour of the system as a whole.

The study of Chaos demonstrates that in complex systems a very small change in any part, as a result of external stress (such as the increase of average world temperature by one degree centigrade), can have results which are unpredictable in both scale and effect (El Nino, floods, droughts and so on). These systems, which have a strong sense of 'self', adapt to the change by finding a new stability. These are known as complex adaptive systems and are hard to destabilise. Much of the organic world falls into this category. This process of stress followed by adaptation is essential for continued survival.

One intriguing result is that complex adaptive systems can evolve into something that has a different behaviour to the original, and that this evolution is unpredictable. Therefore a system can naturally exploit a change in its environment or survive in a niche that it previously did not occupy. This can only happen when the system can adapt freely around its knowledge of 'self'.

Understanding how these systems are created and sustained, and viewing an organisation as a complex adaptive system, has generated new thinking on leadership, thinking which borrows from the past, synthesises the future and makes sense of today.

The next chapter outlines the five circles of influence that need to operate together when creating and leading a modern adaptive organisation, of whatever size. The remaining chapters provide the practical tools and techniques that will enable you as leaders to lead, and to lead well.

# Chapter 2
# A leadership model

**STEP 1**
Thinking
like
a leader

**STEP 2**
Creating
a vision

**STEP 3**
Choosing
a set
of values

**STEP 4**
Recognising
that people
are different

**STEP 5**
Achieving
extraordinary
results

**The five circles
of influence**

To step into leadership, there are five circles of influence of which you must be aware and on which you must take action. Although we have numbered them they are not a sequence, each relates to all the others and taking action in one will inevitably affect the others. We have used five circles as a simple picture of the movement and changeability of the whole.

We suggest that you read the short summaries which follow and then, on a piece of paper, draw your five circles and write in each one what relevant action you have taken in the last week or the last month. When you have completed your lists, redraw the circles to show how much time you have spent on each. For example, if you happen to have spent two days at workshops developing a new corporate vision that circle would be large and, if you haven't given your or the organisation's values any attention recently, that one might be just a dot. Repeat the process for any recent period that makes sense in your current job.

Now look at what you have drawn and ask yourself whether what you see appears to be out of balance. The circles need not be the same size; indeed it would be very odd if that were the case all the time. The picture is there only to give you some information about how you are choosing to spend your time. If you continually ignore one circle you will probably find that there may well be difficulties looming sooner or later. Forewarned is forearmed.

### First circle – thinking like a leader

Leaders are alive to the possibilities of changing things for the better. They are willing to take the responsibility for making the change happen.

Because leadership depends on the cooperation of others, effective leaders know who they are, why they are the way that they are and how they impact on others. They are realists who do not pretend to be good at everything, they are open to challenge and welcome ideas from others. This requires a well-developed sense of self that can only be built through developing reliable self-awareness and feedback from others.

### Second circle – creating a vision

Effective leaders are those who truly understand where they are heading and what they want to achieve.

A vision is a call to the imagination to make a difference. A vision paints a picture of the future. It implies a calling to a cause that is higher than one's self – examples could include a service for a community, a product that will be of benefit to humankind, the protection of ecological resources, or the nurturing of a child.

Many organisations have 'a vision statement' in the foyer to which managers point when asked. Yet influencing through vision means making the vision real for the person you are talking to right now, enabling that person to understand how his or her work helps take the organisation forward.

### Third circle – choosing a set of values

Leaders need a set of values to guide them on the journey.

A set of values provides a lighthouse, a compass and a sounding board to keep us focused and on the right path when the going inevitably gets tough. This value set enables us to test and assess every important leadership decision we make. Examples could include courage, compassion, humility, wisdom or justice.

### Fourth circle – recognising that people are different

People are different and although any two people may arrive at the same conclusion from a set of facts, each may have begun the thinking process in a different place and have given different weights to parts of the information. This difference in approach can lead to mutual irritation if it is not understood and consequently to a reduction in effectiveness in the team.

To motivate and communicate effectively with different people and to increase performance in your organisation you need to develop your understanding, using some new skills and capabilities, and be willing to stand in the other person's shoes.

### Fifth circle – achieving extraordinary results

Think of results in the following terms:

→ for myself
→ for my team
→ for my organisation.

Leadership involves continually checking into the other four stages of the model to ask yourself:

1 Do I want, desire or need to step into this leadership role that has emerged?
2 Do I have the right vision and can I inspire others to pursue it?
3 Do I have the right value set to pursue this vision?
4 Do I have the right skills and attributes to motivate very different people in the leadership role envisaged?
5 If I haven't, how can I develop them?

This circle contains the bulk of the 'doing' of the leadership job. The tips cover all the common challenges which crop up, with proven techniques to handle them. So whether it is how to have a difficult conversation at work or preparing yourself for top positions in the organisation this book will provide the basic information you need and will point to where you can find out more.

**The five circles in practice**

The five steps in the model can be applied to individual leaders, to teams and to organisations.

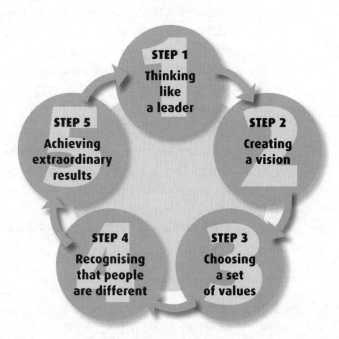

Because leadership can exist only when followers are prepared to follow, the model is in continual flow. Achieve an extraordinary result in step 5 and almost immediately there is a need to embrace step 1 again as the next leadership challenge emerges.

Leadership is continuous, you never reach the point at which it is complete. Every leadership action has an effect on followers and often these effects cannot be predicted. As forensic scientists say, 'every contact leaves a trace'. This applies to leadership in that people remember what a leader did in situations that were important to them. It may be a positive memory or a negative one and they will remember the action and the effect for longer than the leader will be able to recall it.

No leadership situation is the same because people and their motivations are different. It therefore requires a curiosity about people and continual learning to be effective.

---

*Leadership and learning are indispensable to each other.*

J.F. Kennedy, former US President

---

# Chapter **3**
# Thinking like a leader

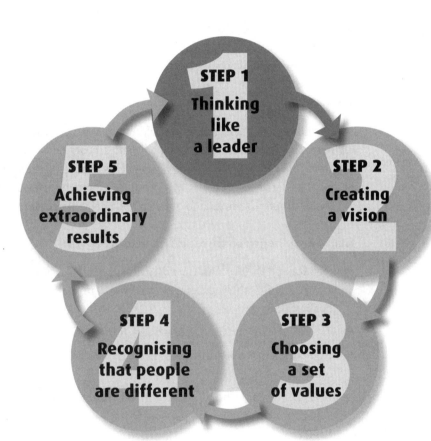

**STEP 1**
Thinking
like
a leader

**STEP 2**
Creating
a vision

**STEP 3**
Choosing
a set
of values

**STEP 4**
Recognising
that people
are different

**STEP 5**
Achieving
extraordinary
results

## Leadership tip **1**
# Begin to THINK like a leader

*Anybody can do a great job when there is nothing at stake. It's when you don't want to do the assignment but you write a great story anyway that you know you are a professional.*

Bob Christopher, Editor, *Newsweek International*

Leaders think differently from others. They believe that they can change something for the better and are willing to take responsibility for making it happen. Leadership involves embracing responsibility where the word 'embrace' means 'to take up readily or gladly'. Anyone can do the glamorous or the sought-after tasks but the real leader is the person who volunteers for the tasks that no one else wants to do and does them in such a way that everyone else wants to help out. Accepting the responsibilities that you are given is not enough. You have to be the one who steps forward and says 'I want to do that'. You can't be a leader if you are afraid of responsibility and accountability.

In order to behave as a leader, an individual must believe that they are, or can become, a leader. Being aware of who you are, of how you are perceived by others and acting on that information helps to develop the strong sense of self all leaders need. Leaders are optimists – their cup is always half-full, never half-empty – they tend to be eager and cheerful people.

**In order to begin to think like a leader:**

→ Look for and think about the positive aspects of the situation you are facing – they do exist – even if you cannot readily identify them.

→ Have your team create a list of what is going right.

→ Always look for opportunities to say 'Yes'. Say 'Yes and…' rather than 'Yes but…'

→ Never lie to people, but do make light of the realities you are facing. An ability to laugh, particularly at yourself, makes others laugh too.

→ Smiling can be overdone, but smiling in the face of adversity disarms most people and cheers up the rest.

→ Create fun out of a situation, and the time in adversity passes more quickly.

→ If you have nothing complimentary to say, say nothing at all unless the situation calls for correction.

→ Be an encourager, not a critic.

→ Accept a compliment gracefully.

→ Praise others. Try to write a handwritten thank-you note to someone every day.

→ Think yourself lucky and tell people that you are lucky. They will tell others that you are lucky and you will become known as a lucky person.

Use your leadership position in a positive way. You are the leader because you know what you are doing and have the vision.

## *In practice...*

*The only day I ever saw John miserable was the day he was made redundant from the steel works in Birkenhead where he was a shop steward. And this misery only lasted 24 hours. On every other occasion he and I met, and there were many of them because we played cricket together for 20 years, he was cheerful and optimistic.*

*After he was made redundant this ex-shop steward from the steel works went for interview for a sales job in the emerging mobile telephone industry. His interviewer described him as a breath of fresh air. He is now a senior manager in BT and still bowling his left arm spinners.*

In order to develop the self-belief to step forward to take a leadership role, potential leaders need a clear picture of what the role involves. Ask yourself these questions:

1  Do I want, desire or need to step into this leadership role that has emerged?

2  Do I have the right vision and can I inspire others to pursue it?

3  Do I have the right value set to pursue this vision?

4  Do I have the right skills and attributes to motivate very different people in the leadership role envisaged?

5  If I haven't, how can I develop them?

6  Do I fully understand all the approaches to leadership that have been developed throughout history?

→ the qualities or traits approach to leadership;

→ the knowledge-based approach to the subject;

→ the functional, behavioural or action-centred approach;

→ the dyadic or relationship-based approach;

→ the contingency or situational approach;

→ the constitutive or visionary approach.

## Read around

*Leadership theory and practice*, R. Daft

## Links to other leadership tips

## Leadership tip **2**

# Identify what you want to CHANGE or how to spot what is WRONG

It is sometimes difficult to recognise what could be improved in your organisation when you are up to your armpits in alligators, fighting to complete the day-to-day tasks for which you are responsible.

What in your work environment do you think needs changing for the better?

→ Are the staff committed and enthusiastic? What is the absenteeism record?

→ Do all the departments cooperate or do they compete internally?

→ Is the product range flying off the shelves or are sales slow and sluggish?

→ Is the work environment conducive to having fun at work?

→ What are the measures you use for customer service and quality? Are they the right ones and what are these measures telling you?

→ Are people leaving the organisation?

→ Should the company be doing more for the community or the environment or to raise money for charity?

→ Etc. etc.

*The absence of alternatives clears the mind marvellously.*

Henry Kissinger, statesman

All the above could indicate things that need improving. You then have to decide whether you want to take the responsibility and accountability for improving things.

**There are three things to remember:**

**1** Never pick a fight with your boss.

**2** Prepare, prepare and prepare some more to make your business case about what needs changing and what the changes should be.

**3** Get your timing right.

**Get your timing right**

It is vitally important to recognise a rising tide. Making a case for change which no one else wants is a futile exercise, like swimming against an ebb tide.

Timing may be the most important element in the alchemy of leadership. Tony Blair was at his best when Princess Diana died and he judged the national mood perfectly with his brilliant populist expression of grief.

Military leaders like Guy Gibson, who led the raids on the dams of the rivers in Germany in the Second World War, spoke of '… never knowing a finer moment. It was as if everything that had gone before was simply preparation and that all that followed was anti-climax'. There is luck in being in the right place at the right time to become famous as a leader.

### In practice…

*Mayor Giuliani in New York pulled off one of the most spectacular leadership reversals of all time. He was not popular among his constituents and he was coming to the end of his uneventful term of office. However, he became a leader overnight after the destruction of the World Trade Center. He announced no new policies, implemented no new tactics but by being in the right place at the right time and doing the right thing, he rode the moral populism of the time. Timing in leadership is sometimes everything.*

However, successful leadership is not a matter of luck. There may be some luck involved in getting the timing so right that one becomes famous for a leadership success. But this is no different from having the luck to become famous as a mountaineer, or an author or an entrepreneur.

Jim Collins in his book *Good to great* describes the research his team undertook to unearth the secrets of the leaders of companies who had sustained their success over many decades. The team found that long-term success and transformation from a good organisation to a great one was the result of leadership from people who were ruthless in their pursuit of the good of their organisation rather than themselves. These leaders were all virtually unknown to the general public.

Collins says of them, 'We were surprised, shocked really, to discover the type of leadership required for turning a good company into a great one. Compared to high profile leaders with big personalities who make the headlines and become celebrities, the good-to-great leaders seem to have come from Mars. Self-effacing, quiet, reserved, even shy – these leaders are a paradoxical blend of personal humility and professional will'.

*Successful leaders are more like Lincoln and Socrates than Patton and Caesar.*

Jim Collins, author

### Read around

*Good to great*, J. Collins

*Leadership*, R. Giuliani

### Links with other tips

# Convince yourself that PEOPLE are key

$$I \times P = E$$

**I** = the leadership initiative you are planning to bring about.

**P** = the people you need to bring home the bacon.

**I** and **P** multiply to give **E**, where **E** = the excellence of the benefits we obtain.

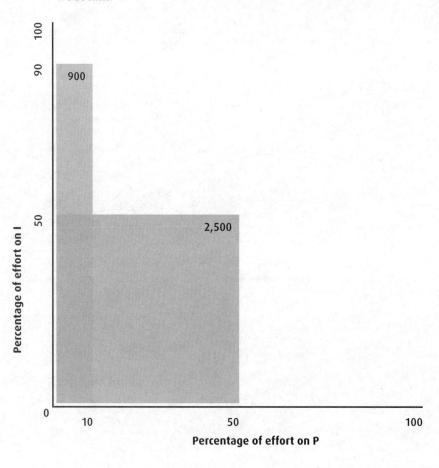

## *In practice...*

*If you put 90% of your effort into the initiative you want to bring about, I will equal 90. And if you put 10% of your effort into your people, P will equal 10. If we multiply I × P, E will equal 900.*

*If you put 50% of your effort in to the initiative and 50% into the people, and multiply I × P, E will equal 2,500 – a return that is almost three times better.*

*If you put no effort into your people, P will equal zero and the result we obtain by multiplying I × P will be zero.*

Leadership is all about people. Whether you are aiming to implement a new strategic direction, a quality improvement initiative, a reorganisation or rebuilding of your business, or a mobilisation of your corporate values, people are the key.

If you put more of your percentage leadership effort on what has to be done and less on the people who have to do it, the poorer the benefits you will get. If you put equal percentage leadership effort into the people who have to do it and into what has to be done, the benefits you will get will be dramatically better. If you put no effort into your people, no matter how hard you work at systems and processes, the result will be zero. In fact the result will be worse than zero because you will have expended time and energy, which has an opportunity for no result.

Source: With acknowledgement to George Eckes, *Making six sigma last*

## *Read around*

*Making six sigma last*, G. Eckes

## *Links to other leadership tips*

**1**   Begin to think like a leader

**27**   Value the differences in people

**28**   Recognise the differences in people

# Tell the difference between MANAGEMENT and leadership

Managers work with processes, models and systems – things. Leaders work with people, relationships and their emotions.

Managers ask 'How can I do things right?' whereas leaders ask 'What are the right things to do and why are they the right things to do?'.

| Management | Leadership |
|---|---|
| Reacting to the expected | Being proactive in all situations |
| Using the left side of the brain | Using the right side of the brain |
| Efficiency | Effectiveness |
| Making the present more tolerable | Inspiring the hope that the future can be better than the present |
| Productivity and quality | Energy, vitality and passion |
| Predicting the future from the past | Inventing the future from the future |
| Implementation | Integrity |
| Drills and procedures | Vision and a call to the imagination |
| Strategies | A set of beliefs and values |
| Budgeting and planning | Non-linear results |

*Good leaders are people who make things happen, as opposed to those who simply administrate.*

Colin Chase, consultant to The Industrial Society

This is not intended to imply that management is bad and that leadership is good. Both are needed for organisational effectiveness. Most leaders are anxious to change things because they can see a future that is better than today. Most managers want to keep things the same because that means a smooth-running operation.

Management without leadership is like a map without a compass, leadership without management is like a compass without a map. Being an ideas person is fine, but not at the expense of reality. Visionary leaders don't actually lead unless they take the necessary steps to implement their vision. Likewise managers can't take the steps they are so good at unless they know in which direction to go.

## In practice...

*Dave spent most of his days as the manager of his department tied to the computer screen and the telephone. He rarely saw his staff or spoke to them. He concentrated on measurement of outputs and results. He did not concentrate his efforts on his people. Dave was a manager not a leader.*

*As a consequence his experienced staff all left over time; the new recruits could not cut the mustard. Finally Dave was given his own marching orders.*

## Read around

*The leadership mystique*, M. Kets de Vries

## Links to other leadership tips

**5**   Recognise that the right hemisphere of the brain is needed for leadership

**38**  Develop the right side of your brain

**95**  Generate fun at work

# Recognise that the RIGHT hemisphere of the BRAIN is needed for leadership

In 1962 Roger Sperry won a Nobel Prize for identifying that the two hemispheres of the brain were the homes to different intellectual functions. Positron Emission Tomography and Magnetic Resonance Imaging now allow scientists to identify the part of the brain that is activated when we perform an action or experience an emotion. They can identify which half of the brain is functioning. The scientific conclusions are:

*Manage from the left, lead from the right.*

Steven Covey, self-development guru, author

| Left-hand side of the brain | Right-hand side of the brain |
| --- | --- |
| Right side of the body | Left side of the body |
| Details | Whole picture |
| Analysis | Visualisation |
| Systems and logic | Intuition |
| Vocabulary | Ideas |
| Facts | Imagination |
| Short-term memory | Long-term memory |
| Criticism | Creativity |

Although people use both sides of the brain, one hemisphere is usually dominant. This means that we all tend to stay with what we are used to and use the dominant hemisphere. Western education concentrates almost entirely on the development of the left-hand side of the brain – words, measurement and logic are respected and admired. Creativity, intuition, sensing and the artistic sides of our abilities tend to be subordinated.

The left hemisphere is vital for efficient management but the right hemisphere is needed for effective leadership. In order to persuade and influence others we need to be able to visualise a future that does not currently exist, to think up creative solutions to problems and to be able to sense when others are struggling or feeling low.

## Read around

*The seven habits of highly effective people,* S. Covey

*The X & Y of leadership,* L. Cook and B. Rothwell

## Links to other leadership tips

# Leadership tip **6**

# Use the QUALITIES or traits approach to leadership

This approach purports to answer the question 'What does a leader have to *be* to be successful?'. This in turn led to the examination of the qualities of great leaders. In 1940 Bird identified 79 qualities that were important to aspiring leaders. In the 1950s the US Armed Forces commissioned a study that distinguished more than 1,600 necessary traits for its officers.

In 1975 the Industrial Society published its first researched list of leadership traits; it polled 175 executives and boiled their responses down to 15 traits, which are shown in the table below. One third of the executives polled concluded that all 15 traits were vital.

| Judgement | Drive | Fairness |
| --- | --- | --- |
| Initiative | Human relations skills | Ambition |
| Integrity | Decisiveness | Dedication |
| Foresight | Dependability* | Objectivity |
| Energy | Emotional stability | Cooperativeness |

*147 definitions of 'dependability' were received

In the period 1950 to 1975 the qualities approach was heavily criticised by leadership thinkers. It was firstly the sheer length of the lists that led others to denigrate this approach. Secondly, none of the lists was consistent and arriving at an agreed list was difficult. Thirdly, no objective definition of a quality such as 'dependability' or 'charisma' could be agreed. Fourthly, no priority order could be decided. Fifthly, each quality or trait looked impossible to measure objectively for appraisal purposes and sixthly, perceived opinion in the 1950s and 1960s was that leadership qualities were not trainable.

For these six reasons the qualities or traits approach fell out of favour for nearly half a century. Only in the 1990s did social scientists and leadership thinkers return to it.

Leadership is about who you are, as well as what you do. It is about values, beliefs and behaviours that all occur naturally and can all be developed. Today, we conclude that personal qualities do matter. Three of the leadership traits that seem essential in any context are self-confidence, honesty plus integrity, and drive.

A leader with a positive self-image and who displays certainty about his or her own ability fosters confidence among followers. Possessing the traits of honesty and integrity is essential to minimise scepticism and to build productive relationships. Leaders with drive seek achievement, have energy and tenacity, and are seen to have the ambition and initiative to achieve their goals.

Those who wish to improve their leadership potential need to develop:

→ a positive self image;

→ complete honesty in all situations;

→ integrity by living and being their word;

→ their drive and determination to achieve the selected goal.

## In practice...

*Sir Clive Woodward as coach of the England rugby team learned that some players sapped the energy from a team by moaning about the conditions, the pressure or the need to change. Others energised the team by being positive and open to new ideas and had the drive to win no matter the personal cost.*

*He wanted energisers not sappers in his team. The energisers are the leaders and he wanted a team full of leaders. His team won the World Cup in 2003.*

## Read around

*Leadership for dummies*, M. Loeb and S. Kindel

*Leadership theory and practice*, R. Daft

*Winning*, Sir Clive Woodward

## Links to other leadership tips

**1** Begin to think like a leader

**18** Decide your own set of values

# Leadership tip **7**
# Use the KNOWLEDGE-based approach

The failure of the early traits-based approaches led researchers to examine what a leader had to *know*. In essence this approach can be summarised as 'Authority flows from the one who knows'. The person who has the most knowledge or skill in the required area should be the leader of the task for the time it takes to solve the problem.

The best place to read about this type of leadership is in daily newspapers. They are full of stories of people who had the right amount of knowledge and responded to the circumstances to fulfil a leadership role. It may have been a rescue, an accident or dealing with an injury, but the person with the right amount of knowledge appeared at the right time to lead.

*The Australians select the best team of cricketers and then choose the captain from amongst those selected.*

Mike Brearley, former England cricket captain, author, psychotherapist

### In practice...

*Applying this theory to the world of work means appointing or electing the leader with the most knowledge to suit the situation when the time is right. Whatever the status or the experience of the team members in other walks of life, the person appropriate to skipper a yacht is the person who has passed the examinations to obtain a yacht master's certificate. Following this logic through, if a team from one commercial organisation goes sailing for the weekend and the junior clerk is the skipper, the junior clerk will have the leadership right to request the managing director to clean the heads.*

At work, most team, department or divisional leaders are appointed, or at least ratified, from above. When appointing people for leadership roles some organisations follow this knowledge-based dictum unwittingly. They promote the best secretary to be the office supervisor, the best sales person to be the sales manager, the most reliable accountant to be the accounts section leader, or the best cricketer to be the captain.

Knowledge-based leadership does have its place in the changing workplace of this new twenty-first century. Leadership can be rotated within a team, so that the most appropriate person to lead a project is given the opportunity to lead irrespective of organisational status and experience. Others in the team give leadership advice, help and guidance within the team.

This has the advantages of:

→ matching skills to project requirements;

→ developing leadership throughout the team to the benefit of both team and individuals;

→ sharing the leadership load;

→ allowing more experienced leaders to practise coaching those less inexperienced.

## Read around

*The action centred leader*, J. Adair

*The art of captaincy*, M. Brearley

## Links to other leadership tips

**8** Use the functional, behavioural or action-centred approach to leadership

**39** Use business performance coaching

# Use the FUNCTIONAL, behavioural or ACTION-CENTRED approach to leadership

The disadvantages of the qualities and the knowledge-based approaches led leadership thinkers in the 1960s to ask themselves the question, 'What does a leader have to *do*?'.

In 1964, at Sandhurst, when involved with training military officers, John Adair came up with the memorable leadership model below in answer to this question. And in so doing he invented the functional approach to leadership.

*Through doing, you become.*

John Garnett, Director, The Industrial Society, 1962–86

The objective is to keep the three circles in balance over time. A good leader will put as much effort into building the team as she does into achieving the task and developing individuals. Neglect in any one of the circles will lead to a leadership failure.

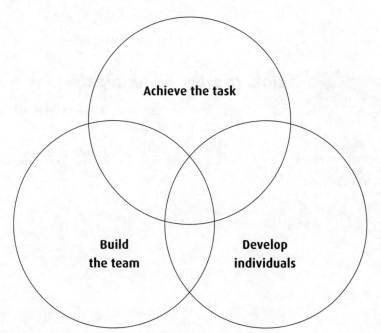

Opposite is the standard leadership checklist of tasks set out by Dr John Adair. They are as relevant today as the day he first penned them. All leaders could benefit by using this checklist to ensure that all the necessary actions have been taken.

For those who can remember being ACL (Action Centred Leadership) trained, it involved appointing a leader of a team to accomplish a task. That task was to complete a jigsaw, build a tower of Lego bricks or watch a film called *Twelve o'clock high*. The leaders were appraised using the checklist below.

| Key actions | Task | Team | Individual |
|---|---|---|---|
| Define objectives | Identify task and constraints | Share commitment | Gain acceptance |
| Plan | Check resources | Consult | Encourage ideas Assess skills |
| Decide | Agree priorities and standards | Structure | Allocate jobs Delegate Agree targets |
| Communicate | Clarify objectives | Explain decisions Answer questions Check understanding | Listen Enthuse |
| Monitor | Assess progress | Coordinate | Discipline |
| Support | Maintain standards | | Deal with grievance Assist, reassure |
| Evaluate | Review Re-plan | Guide Train | Give praise |

## Read around

*The action centred leader*, J. Adair

*The work challenge*, J. Garnett

## Links to other leadership tips

**16**  Think creatively

**35**  Analyse problems

**53**  Really listen

**71**  Communicate openly

**72**  Consult those affected before making a decision

**79**  Give praise

# Leadership tip **9**

# Use the DYADIC or RELATIONSHIP-based approach to leadership

### *In practice...*

*John Buchan, the novelist, gave one of the first formal lectures on leadership in Britain in 1930 at St Andrews University. For Buchan, the task of leadership was not to put greatness into people, but to elicit the greatness that was already there. For the first time this speech put the emphasis not just on the role of the leader but also on the role of the followers. It is the people who are led who make the leader.*

*Concentrate on the relationship for the sake of the relationship, not on what you want to get out of the relationship.*

Mikki Walleczek, entrepreneur, sailor, guru

Dyadic theorists believe that the trait and behaviour approaches oversimplify the relationship between leaders and followers. They focus on the concept of an exchange between the leader and follower, a relationship known as a dyad. The word dyad stems from the Greek language and means the number two, a group of two, a couple.

The dyadic view is that a single leader will form different relationships with different followers. For example, interviewing different subordinates of a leader at work will reveal different descriptions of the same person, with some descriptions being positive and some negative. Leadership profiling and 360-degree appraisal schemes provide the evidence that individual followers view the same leader in different ways.

The first academic dyadic theory was produced over 25 years ago and has been steadily revised ever since. Today it has developed to the point shown in the model opposite.

1. **Vertical dyad linkage**
Leaders' behaviours and traits
have different effects
on each individual follower

2. **Leader-follower exchange**
Leadership is individualised
for each follower. Each dyad involves a unique
exchange independent of other dyads

3. **Partnership building**
Leaders can reach out to create a positive
exchange with each follower.
Doing so increases performance

4. **Systems and networks**
Leader dyads can be created in all directions
across levels and boundaries to build networks
that enhance performance

Studies of leadership in sport always provide the evidence that athletes
have to be treated in different ways by the captain or coach in order to
produce the fulfilment of their talent. Leadership will always depend on
the quality of the relationships that leaders can form with followers and
others. Leaders will always be good networkers.

## Read around

*A simpler way*, M. Wheatley and M. Kellner-Rogers

*How to win friends and influence people*, D. Carnegie

*Leadership theory and practice*, R. Daft

## Links to other leadership tips

**26** Use distinction-based learning

**27** Value the differences in people

**28** Recognise the differences in people

**56** Network as a leader

## Leadership tip **10**

# Use the CONTINGENCY or SITUATIONAL approach to leadership

*There is a tide in the affairs of men, which, taken at the flood leads on to fortune.*

William Shakespeare,
*Julius Caesar*

The traits, knowledge-based and dyadic approaches all sought universal solutions that could be applied in all situations. The contingent approach implies that one thing depends on another. In a leadership sense there must be an appropriate fit between the leader's behaviour and the situation in which the leader is operating and the followers involved. In other words, leadership never happens in isolation.

### In practice...

*History is littered with examples of men who led very success-fully for a period, a season or a war and then were rejected by the people they wanted to lead. Winston Churchill, Margaret Thatcher and Mikhail Gorbachev are but three examples.*

Contingency theorists state that we need to examine not only the make up of the leader but also the make up of the followers and the specifics of the situation in which they find themselves.

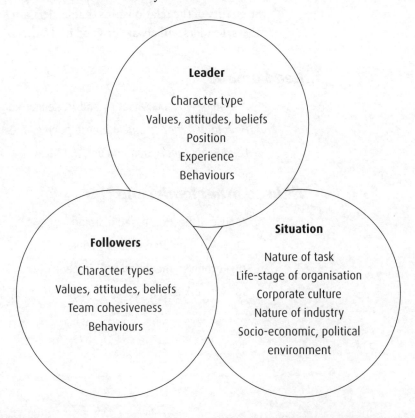

**Leader**

Character type
Values, attitudes, beliefs
Position
Experience
Behaviours

**Followers**

Character types
Values, attitudes, beliefs
Team cohesiveness
Behaviours

**Situation**

Nature of task
Life-stage of organisation
Corporate culture
Nature of industry
Socio-economic, political
environment

An effective leader will understand

→ the current situation and the needs of the organisation;

→ the people, their skills and their interaction;

→ his/her own impact and preferred style.

And the leader will choose the most appropriate style to enable the followers to complete the chosen task. Effective leadership is therefore about developing diagnostic skills to be able to judge the readiness of the followers to achieve the task, and then being flexible enough to move from one style to another.

### Use of authority in decision-making

**Leader centred**                                           **Team centred**

| Leader decides and announces decision | Leader sells decision to team | Leader announces decision, then permits questions | Leader presents tentative decision, consults team and then decides | Leader presents problem, asks for ideas, and then decides |
|---|---|---|---|---|

## Read around

*Management of organisational behaviour, utilising human resources,* P. Hersey and K. Blanchard

*Mastering leadership,* M. Williams

## Links to other leadership tips

**63** Recognise that your habitual leadership style is ineffective or becoming stale

# Leadership tip **11**

## Use the CONSTITUTIVE or visionary approach to leadership

Constitutive theory is derived from the new sciences, metaphysics, biology and fuzzy logic. It involves viewing an organisation as a complex adaptive system. Complexity Theory is used to investigate complex systems such as living organisms, the weather or evolution. We now know that it is the interaction of these components, the sharing of knowledge between them, which controls the structure and behaviour of the complex system as a whole.

The study of Chaos demonstrates that in complex systems a very small change in any part, as a result of external stress, can have results that are unpredictable in both scale and effect. These systems, which have a strong sense of 'self', adapt to the change by finding a new stability. These are known as complex adaptive systems and are hard to destabilise. Much of the organic world falls into this category.

Constitutive theory states that a leader's role is to turn visionary ideas into a story that those involved can relate to, make sense of and understand. It is the job of the leader to paint a picture of the future that is better than the present or the past. Leaders are not paid for the continuation of what is there already, nor are they paid for what is going to happen anyway, those are the jobs of managers. Leaders are paid to sense what is missing and then to invent something to fill this gap.

*Insanity is doing the same old things in the same old ways and expecting different results.*

Rita Mae Brown, actress

→ Formulate and communicate a shared vision and values that have been crafted with care.

→ Coach and guide by shared vision, values, rules and consequences; bearing in mind that people aren't perfect!

→ Develop shared meanings throughout the organisation.

→ Build a fabric of relationships and mutuality. Be more concerned with enabling the interplay between people than the outcomes of their work.

→ Influence the number of interactions between people (inside and outside the organisation) and increase them wherever possible.

→ Be a purveyor of enthusiasm about everything for which the organisation stands.

→ Put more effort into knowledge capture and sharing than into operational processes.

→ Enable the behaviours the organisation wants, rather than the outcomes.

→ Create the possibility to experiment. Enable the unauthorised.

→ Nurture the formation of diverse teams and let them evolve solutions. Seek diversity of people across genders, cultures, expertise, ages and personalities.

→ Replace 'central control' with clarity of accountability.

→ Enable everyone in the organisation to see how their work contributes to the success of the whole.

→ Dismantle anything that runs contrary to the above.

## In practice...

*Richard Livesey-Haworth used the above checklist to formulate the reorganisation of The Industrial Society in a process that was called 'The Smart Design'. It took the whole of 2000 and was successful.*

## Read around

*Chaos, the amazing science of the unpredictable*, J. J. Gleick

*Leadership and the new sciences*, M. Wheatley

## Links to other leadership tips

**12** Create a vision for your own operation

**24** Create a set of team or organisational values

**39** Use business performance coaching

**61** Be a servant leader

67

# Chapter 4
# Creating a vision

STEP 1
Thinking
like
a leader

STEP 2
Creating
a vision

STEP 3
Choosing
a set
of values

STEP 4
Recognising
that people
are different

STEP 5
Achieving
extraordinary
results

# Leadership tip **12**

# CREATE A VISION for your own operation

A business vision provides followers with the hope that the future will be better than the present. Leaders should be in the business of providing their people with hope. And it is more than that. Having a clear idea of how things could be and the direction in which the organisation is heading enables everyone to make small day-to-day decisions to move towards the big picture.

### Definition

A vision is an ambitious dream that is communicable, memorable, achievable, sustainable and inspirational. It is not measurable.

A vision is like a:

→ **Compass** – it gives us clear direction by binding people together in the hope of fulfilling a common purpose.

→ **Dynamo** – it generates energy and enthusiasm.

→ **Sounding board** – it resonates with the values and aspirations of all in the organisation.

→ **Beacon** – it shines to show us the way to go.

### When creating a vision, do…

1 Encourage and engage your imagination.

2 Create the vision in the present tense so as to reinforce the sense of 'being in the midst of it'.

3 Be prepared to 'unlearn' and to suspend preconceptions.

4 Accept that your first efforts may seem 'naff'.

5 Brainstorm the ingredients of the vision with your team. These are best expressed in single words, not phrases or sentences.

**6** Ask the participants to describe what they see and feel when contemplating the vision, for example:

| See | Feel |
|---|---|
| → Delighted clients | → Pride |
| → Fulfilled colleagues | → Energy |
| → Harmony among stakeholders | → Wider sense of purpose |
| → Strong demand for services | → Achievement |
| → Potential recruits eager to join | → Happiness in being part of it |

**7** Experiment with imagery – 'Broad sunlit uplands' (Churchill) or 'Land of milk and honey' (Old Testament).

**8** Use simple terms that people recognise, relate to and remember – 'I have a dream' (Martin Luther King).

**9** Invite challenge from colleagues at all levels to create wider ownership and impact.

**10** Give the vision time to mature – you will nearly always be able to improve on the first version(s).

**11** Test the vision – 'What, if anything, does X or Y have to do with our vision?'.

**12** The vision, though not measurable itself, must be clearly linked to measurable objectives.

**Do not...**

**1** Confuse vision with intention. A vision should not start with the word 'To'.

**2** Use jargon.

**3** Impose your interpretation of the vision on others, but rather encourage them to interpret it for themselves.

**4** Try to compromise by combining unrelated ideas.

**5** Fudge by using words like 'best' – they endanger credibility and seldom inspire.

**6** Substitute a vision for measurable planning.

Source: Ben Thompson-McCausland, lecturer, coach

## In practice. . .

*'We are ladies and gentlemen serving ladies and gentlemen.'*

*Europa Hotel, Belfast.*

*'Absolutely, positively, overnight.'* Federal Express

*'Winning.'* England rugby union elite squad under Sir Clive Woodward

The vision embraces more than the literal words it contains. To those involved, the vision can mean many things – and they are the things that they decide it means. For example the Europa Hotel vision embraces standards of courtesy, service and timeliness that we find uncommon in the hotel trade. The staff however all know what the vision means. The vision of the England RFU elite squad embraces not only more points on the scoreboard but also a stadium of 75,000 people going nuts about the way the team plays.

It is a common preconception that a vision can only be constructed from the top of an organisation. We disagree. If your organisation has a vision and it is a good one, you may like to link the vision of your area of operations to it. If it is a mediocre one, you may wish to ignore it when creating a vision for your own department. If your organisation does not have a vision, please do not use this as an excuse not to formulate one for your people. They need the hope that tomorrow can be better than today, irrespective of the actions of the rest of the organisation.

## Read around

*Inspirational leadership*, R. Olivier

*Winning*, Sir Clive Woodward

## Links to other leadership tips

**13** Evaluate the current vision for your operation

**14** Identify behaviours that fit the vision

**15** Use a vision to develop your organisation

**16** Think creatively

**17** Think creatively in teams

# Leadership tip **13**

# EVALUATE THE CURRENT VISION for your operation

Four necessary characteristics for a vision are that it should be short, achievable or doable, memorable and inspirational. Four more are that it should act as a compass, a dynamo and a beacon, and it should resonate with our values.

Whether you have inherited a vision from elsewhere or you have created one, here is a simple checklist to evaluate it.

**Evaluate your vision**

Let each team member fill in the form; giving their own opinion. Zero represents a poor match between your vision and the necessary characteristic. Five is a perfect match between the vision and the characteristic.

Then in a team meeting sum and average the scores. Unless you have an average score above 3.5 for each necessary characteristic, you have more work to do on the vision for your area of the operation.

| Necessary characteristic | 0 | 1 | 2 | 3 | 4 | 5 |
|---|---|---|---|---|---|---|
| Short | | | | | | |
| Achievable | | | | | | |
| Memorable | | | | | | |
| Inspirational | | | | | | |
| A compass giving clear direction | | | | | | |
| A dynamo generating enthusiasm | | | | | | |
| A beacon showing the way | | | | | | |
| Resonating with our values | | | | | | |

## *Links to other leadership tips*

**12** Create a vision for your own operation

**14** Identify behaviours that fit the vision

**15** Use a vision to develop your organisation

**16** Think creatively

**17** Think creatively in teams

## Leadership tip **14**
# Identify BEHAVIOURS THAT FIT THE VISION

*The future is now.*

Old saying

It is essential to make the vision actionable and, to do this, undertake the 'bull's eye' exercise. This enables us to go from the broad-brush approach of establishing the vision using the right side of the brain, through the mindset changes that will be needed to use the left brain to produce actionable behaviours.

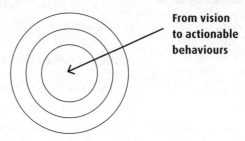

From vision to actionable behaviours

### Behaviour that will make your vision reality

In order to bring the vision into being, identify the behaviours that you will need from all parts of the organisation. For example, you may need more details from service providers prior to tender, more responsiveness from personnel to fill outstanding vacancies, more budget from finance or more support from the chief executive.

Then consider what behaviours you want less of and list them. For example, you may want fewer last-minute requests from finance, less insistence from personnel that your people attend residential courses or less interference from service providers as tenders are worked on.

#### Example

**Vision** Every tender on time

**Behaviours**

| **More of:** | **Less of:** |
|---|---|
| 1 Details from service providers prior to tender | 1 Last minute requests from finance |
| 2 Responsiveness from personnel to fill outstanding vacancies | 2 Interference from service providers as tenders are worked upon |
| 3 Budget | 3 Insistence from HR that people attend residential courses |
| 4 Support from CEO | |

### Read around

*Greg Dyke, inside story*, G. Dyke

### Links to other leadership tips

# Leadership tip **15**

# Use a VISION to develop your organisation

A leader recognises that the performance of the organisation depends on getting everyone to work together to move things forward. Working together happens naturally when people share the same vision of what the organisation is for and how their individual contributions fit into the overall picture.

The starting point is to have a shared idea of what could be – a **vision**.

The next step is to decide what the goals are, which, when accomplished, fulfil the vision. This is the **mission** and it is measurable.

Both vision and mission are long-term aspirations.

The **strategic direction** (or strategic plan) sets out in more detail, over the medium term, those priorities which need to be achieved in order to fulfil the mission.

The annual **business plan** provides the detail of the goals which will be delivered to move in the strategic direction.

And **team and individual performance agreements** set out the specific responsibilities and accountabilities of everyone in the organisation which, cumulatively, deliver the annual business plan.

Taken together, these linked plans allow each person in the organisation to have a clear line of sight from his or her day job to the organisational vision and to understand how individual contributions fit and matter to the whole.

They provide the means to achieve mutual agreement and understanding between all team members and the leader about what is to be done, how it is to be done and the direction in which the team and the organisation is heading.

### *In practice...*

**Vision** – *an inspirational yet doable dream:*
*'Absolutely, positively overnight.' FedEx*
*'We are ladies and gentlemen serving ladies and gentlemen.' Europa Hotel, Belfast*

**Mission** – *a statement summarising the goals that when accomplished, fulfil the vision:*
*'A man on the moon in ten years.' J.F. Kennedy*
*'One third of our turnover to come from new product.' EMI*

**Strategic direction** – *the path from where we are now towards accomplishing the mission:*
*'We are going north from London to Birmingham up the M1.'*
*'I aim to spend three years as an FD before I apply for a CEO job.'*

**Business plan** – *the series of intermediate goals to be achieved this year that respond to the current situation and which accomplish the next steps in the strategic plan:*
*'There is an accident on the M1; we must detour through Coventry via the M45.'*
*'We are going to build the team before we start designing the product.'*

**Team and individual performance agreements** – *the specific goals and actions which the team or individual will deliver this year as their part of the business plan:*
*'15% increase in sales.'*
*'All managers to have leadership training by the year end.'*

A leader needs to refer consistently to the vision, the mission and the direction by linking the benefits of achieving each of the concepts. This will help to reinforce the belief of others in the vision. This needs to done one-to-one, in small groups, in large presentations and in all dealings with the media.

A leader also needs to challenge activities which are underway, perhaps due to history, which do not contribute to delivery of the mission and vision.

## Read around

*Leadership for dummies*, M. Loeb and S. Kindel

## Links to other leadership tips

**12** Create a vision for your own operation

**13** Evaluate the current vision for your operation

**14** Identify behaviours that fit the vision

**16** Think creatively

**17** Think creatively in teams

# THINK CREATIVELY

To come up with a vision that will inspire people and keep them going when things are going badly we need to think creatively. Our experience is limited to the past – our imagination is not. We can stand in the future without the constraints of the present and look backwards. We can use lateral thinking.

## Eight lateral thinking techniques

**1**  Reverse your thinking

Pencils are usually straight. So think of the benefits of having a curved pencil. It would not roll off the desk, it would sit better in the hand, it would go in the bum pocket.

**2**  Exaggerate your thinking

Postage stamps are usually small. Think through the benefits of having A4-sized postage stamps. You could write on them, the stamp could be paper, envelope and stamp all in one.

**3**  Distort your thinking

People usually brush their own teeth. Suppose we cleaned someone else's teeth – what would be the benefits? It is very intimate; could we have teeth cleaning for lovers?

**4**  Object stimulation

Having trouble coming up with your vision? Think of your vision as a clock, a camera, a desk, a helicopter (or any other concrete noun) and the ideas will begin to flow.

**5**  The analogy game

We have a problem merging two corporate cultures after a merger. Imagine our former two companies as two ships; now we are all on the one ship. What are the advantages?

**6**  How would you feel about this if…?

How would you feel about this if you were Nelson Mandela, or Ghandi, or Florence Nightingale?

*The best way to predict the future is to create it.*

Peter Drucker, business guru, author

**7** Wouldn't it be wonderful if…?

Wouldn't it be wonderful if there was a key on the computer keyboard that said F…IT?

**8** Create a rich picture

Let's draw satisfied customers; let's draw our workforce with high morale.

## Read around

*Creativity for managers*, A. Barker

*Handbook for creative team leaders*, T. Rickards and M. Moger

*Lateral thinking*, E. de Bono

## Links to other leadership tips

**12** Create a vision for your own operation

**13** Evaluate the current vision for your operation

**14** Identify behaviours that fit the vision

**15** Use a vision to develop your organisation

**17** Think creatively in teams

## Leadership tip **17**

# THINK CREATIVELY IN TEAMS

The Nominal Group Technique is now widely used in place of classic brainstorming. Because approximately 50% of the population are introverts and the rest extroverts this technique draws on individual and team strengths and can be used for issue identification, idea generation and problem solving.

*Consistency is the last refuge of the unimaginative.*

Oscar Wilde, playwright, author

**Nominal Group Technique**

1   Begin with a carefully crafted **statement of the problem**. Allow participants to seek clarification and to reframe the problem in their own words. However, do not alter the original wording – step 1 is all about forcing people to think through the problem in their own words.

2   This stage is called **silent generation**. Allow approximately 15 minutes for this phase. Each participant is asked to write down his or her own suggestions for solving the problem. Team members should remain within the room as the atmosphere of work encourages concentration.

3   Now the **round robin** stage commences. Each member is asked to put forward in turn one idea or suggestion. These will usually be taken from the list generated in the previous phase but not necessarily so. Often additional ideas will be stimulated by others' ideas. No criticism of an idea is accepted at this stage. All ideas are entered onto a flip chart or charts. Continue untill all ideas have been shared.

4   Next comes the **idea clarification** phase. Again criticism is not allowed. Each idea is further clarified and modified as necessary. The team should also group ideas into similar themes. Draw lines to show the links between ideas – this is known as an affinity diagram. There may be some additions or rephrasing needed at this point. One possibility at this stage is to use creative techniques such as visualisation techniques or alternative words.

5   Then comes **selection and ranking**. Blank cards or post-it notes are issued to team members. Individually and in silence each member is asked to rank the top six suggestions anonymously. Use six for the best idea and one for the least favourite.

**6** The final stage involves the **final ranking**. Each idea will attract a string of numbers (or no numbers at all). Now the scores are added up. In the case of a tie the idea with the most individuals voting for that idea is deemed the higher of the two.

The result is a ranked set of ideas which, even though there may not have been complete team consensus, has at least come close to this ideal and which have been generated without dominance by any team member or personality type.

Source: J. Bichenco, *Quality 75*

## *Read around*

*Quality 75, towards six sigma performance in service and manufacturing,* J. Bichenco

## *Links to other leadership tips*

**12** Create a vision for your own operation

**13** Evaluate the current vision for your operation

**14** Identify behaviours that fit the vision

**15** Use a vision to develop your organisation

**16** Think creatively

# Chapter **5**
# **Choosing a set of values**

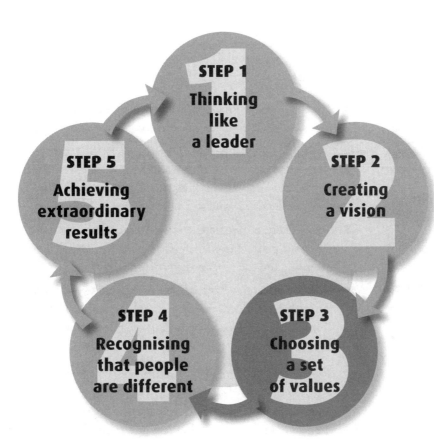

STEP 1
Thinking like a leader

STEP 2
Creating a vision

STEP 3
Choosing a set of values

STEP 4
Recognising that people are different

STEP 5
Achieving extraordinary results

# Leadership tip **18**

# Decide your own SET OF VALUES

Values are the deeply held beliefs that guide our actions or make us feel uneasy or guilty on occasion. We may be aware of some of them, e.g. honesty or reliability, and there may be others which we have not taken time to think about. Being clear about what our personal values are makes it much easier to choose an organisation or job and understand why we get along better with some people than others, and makes saying 'no' much easier.

*One of my values is wisdom. That does not make me a wise man, but it does help me respect wisdom in others and thereby give me an opportunity to learn a little myself.*

Ben Thompson-
McCausland,
businessman, author

## Define your values

1  Think of two or three close friends. Note down the qualities of each that you find most attractive, e.g. sense of humour, always willing to listen.

2  Now ask yourself what each would have to do to end the friendship in your eyes, perhaps making fun of you or your family, breaking your confidence ... and so on. Note these down beside the qualities.

3  Think of one or two people you dislike or who irritate you. Note down the main reason for this, perhaps one doesn't do what he promises and the other gossips behind everyone's back.

4  Now ask yourself what each could do to make you overlook the fault you have noted, perhaps by looking on the positive side of things or being good with difficult people – whatever it will take to make you think that they are not so bad after all.

5  You should find that 1. and 4. suggest similar ideas; in the examples given they would be positive attitude and willingness to listen.

6  Likewise, 2. and 3., being unreliable and untrustworthy might be the common themes so reliability and trustworthiness might be the most important values.

7  Now decide which are the most important to you. You can do this by comparing each with all the others and asking yourself which would matter most if it was broken, e.g. willingness to listen or trustworthiness, willingness to listen or positive attitude.

Repeat this process until you are satisfied with your list of values.

By following the steps outlined opposite you will reach a shortlist of a few values that are very important to you. These are your **core values**. They are the fundamental attitudes which define you and which guide how you act and why.

A list of potential values is shown below.

| | | |
|---|---|---|
| Achievement | Expertise | Personal development |
| Accomplishment | Freedom | Pleasure |
| Adventure | Fun | Power |
| Assertiveness | Generosity | Presence |
| Calmness | Growth | Privacy |
| Challenge | Helping others | Profit |
| Change | Honesty | Quality |
| Commitment | Humility | Recognition |
| Community | Humour | Relationships |
| Competence | Independence | Reputation |
| Confidence | Influence | Resilience |
| Consistency | Integrity | Responsibility |
| Cooperation | Intellect | Security |
| Courage | Involvement | Self-esteem |
| Creativity | Joyfulness | Self-reliance |
| Decisiveness | Judgement | Self-respect |
| Directness | Justice | Stability |
| Discretion | Knowledge | Status |
| Dynamism | Loyalty | Subtlety |
| Effectiveness | Merit | Truth |
| Efficiency | Money | Trust |
| Encouragement | Objectivity | Wealth |
| Enjoyment | Openness | Wisdom |
| Equality | Optimism | Wit |
| Ethics | Order | Wonder |
| Excellence | Patience | Etc… |
| Excitement | Peace | |

### Read around

*Waiting for the mountain to move*, C. Handy

*The hungry spirit*, C. Handy

*When work doesn't work any more: women, work and identity*,
E. P. McKenna

### Links to other leadership tips

**19** Use the set of values that you have created

**20** Reconcile personal values when they don't align with organisational behaviours

**21** Tell when it is time to resign

**22** Set a good example

**23** Keep your promises

**24** Create a set of team or organisational values

**25** Embed new behaviours in line with the values in your organisation

## Leadership tip **19**

# USE THE SET OF VALUES that you have created

Suppose that the personal set of values that you have created is as follows:

→ honesty

→ moral courage

→ wisdom

→ justice

→ humility.

Now suppose that you have a big leadership decision to make that will affect other people, for instance to:

→ close a branch of the operation;

→ choose a new computer supplier;

→ make 20 staff redundant;

→ do business with an organisation the values of which you suspect;

→ stop dealing with a particular client;

→ move the administration function out of London;

→ merge with another organisation.

You can now test the decision you have made against your values by asking whether this is:

→ an honest decision?

→ a courageous decision?

→ a wise decision?

→ a just decision?

→ a humble decision?

If the answer to any of the above is 'No', the decision is not true to your values.

### In practice. . .

*Brian once faced a difficult decision as chairman of a small company. The decision was either to close the operation down or to borrow to give it time to develop its market.*

*He was reminded by a fellow director that the company had established a set of values for the organisation four years previously. One of the values adopted was that of 'being a debt-free company'.*

*The directors reviewed the current situation against this value and all agreed that the company should be closed.*

If the set of values is shared by a team or a board of directors, they can together decide whether the decision is the right one by using the same method. In a team environment it is sometimes useful to get every individual to score the decision against each value on a one to ten scale – with ten perfectly meeting the value and one failing to meet the value at all. The results are then pooled.

### Links to other leadership tips

**18** Decide your own set of values

**20** Reconcile personal values when they don't align with organisational behaviours

**21** Tell when it is time to resign

**22** Set a good example

**23** Keep your promises

**24** Create a set of team or organisational values

**25** Embed new behaviours in line with the values in your organisation

## Leadership tip **20**

# RECONCILE PERSONAL VALUES when they don't align with organisational behaviours

Be sure of your own thinking. Be prepared to take time out to think. This is serious; take it seriously. Distinguish clearly between a non-alignment of values as opposed to a clash of personalities or styles, or a mere disagreement as to what constitutes a non-discretionary task.

→ Make certain that your own values will stand the test of time. Ask yourself – 'Will I still be committed to my values in five years?'.

→ Buy yourself a notebook and dedicate the book to a self-analysis on this issue. Write down feelings as well as facts. Review all that you have written on a regular basis to seek recurring themes and patterns of thinking.

→ Differentiate between the circle of your concerns – which means identifying all the things you are concerned about – and the circle of your influence – those things that you can affect directly. Analyse the size of each. The circle of your influence is usually smaller than the circle of your concerns. You may be able to resolve some issues by concentrating on the things that you can do something about rather than the things you can do nothing about.

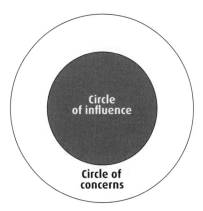

→ Carefully analyse the organisational values. They may not be explicitly stated. Test the validity of this analysis by talking it through with trusted non-involved people.

→ Find the right question (rather than the right answer) and be prepared to 'stand in this question', being open to all possibilities.

→ Consider the possibility that you may be able to change the values of the organisation. Recognise that this will not be easy. Analyse your own skills and attributes and assess whether you could achieve this aim.

→ Put aside all ego-centred thinking that may make you want to be seen to 'look good in the eyes of others' or to 'be right on this issue'.

→ Distinguish your justifications for the way you feel and genuinely try to ignore them.

→ Analyse the effects of your decision on others – your family and friends, colleagues at work and members of your wider community.

**If you come to the crunch there are four options**

**1** You can resign, serve your notice and walk away from the organisation forever.

**2** You can resign, opt not to serve your notice and use this time to plan to take action to change things from outside the organisation.

**3** You can decide to stay put and do nothing – the issue having been resolved in your own mind.

**4** You can decide to stay put and change things from within.

### *In practice...*

*Dan once worked for a charity that relied on the efforts of volunteer labour to coach groups of managers attending their leadership courses.*

*The senior management of the charity decided that they would introduce a bonus scheme for themselves based on the achievement of financial objectives arising from the success of the courses. This offended his values. He could not consider a future with an organisation that asked volunteers to perform for nothing and yet awarded a financial bonus to its senior managers.*

*He quit.*

## *Links to other leadership tips*

# Leadership tip **21**
# **Tell when it is time to RESIGN**

*Falling on your sword is usually the wrong thing to do.*

Andrew Cardew,
Chairman, City PR firm

If a leader in a responsible position has been fraudulent or corrupt then resignation is the only option. If however the difficulty being experienced is an honest and genuine mistake or a non-alignment of values, or the problem has arisen through no fault of your own, to say 'I've had enough – I'm off' rarely serves the interests of other stakeholders.

You are employed by other stakeholders to fight their battles and it is self-indulgent to leave. You may be under pressure and want to produce a quick fix and a pragmatic solution to get the media off your back, but to do so is uncourageous. More difficult, but more honourable and responsible, is to work your guts out to restore some balance to the organisation and then plan your succession.

## When is offering to resign the right thing to do?

→ When you lose the capability or the authority to lead.

→ When you have failed to deliver what you promised.

→ When you have failed to maintain the confidence and trust of the stakeholders.

## How to make the decision

→ Use your values and ask yourself 'Is this a wise decision?', 'Is this a courageous decision?', 'Is this an honest decision?' etc.

→ Get advice. Use your solicitor, your accountant, your investment advisers as well as trusted friends. Listen to their truths. Make a list of the pros and cons for going and for staying. Then decide what to do.

→ If you decide to go, be decisive and act quickly. Use the correct procedures. Write a simple letter alluding to your notice period. Leave the reasons for resignation for the exit interview. Offer to work your notice period and if you are required to do so, run the last lap as hard as you ran the first. Make sure that, if possible, your handover to your successor goes smoothly. Act with honour and dignity in all you do.

→ Learn from the experience as much as possible.

## In practice...

*Josie tells a story of a resignation she made during her career. At that time she was a senior sales manager with a large number of sales staff reporting to her. Despite impressive sales figures, she had continual disagreements with her boss. One day she lost it and resigned. Her boss immediately accepted her decision. The reaction of her staff surprised her. They said 'Who is going to protect us now?'.*

*Josie has never forgotten this and will never again make such a peremptory decision without considering the views of those others affected.*

## Read around

*Kick start your career*, J. Grout and S. Perrin

## Links to other leadership tips

## Leadership tip **22**
# Set a good EXAMPLE

People make the decision to follow a leader through observing what the leader does. It is actions that convince followers, not words. The way you behave as a leader has a vital bearing on your success in the role.

Formulate your own leadership inventory. An example is shown below.

### A leadership inventory

**1 ★ Magician** (see p. 108)

1 Creates a vision for his or her operation
2 Communicates enthusiastically
3 Sees and communicates the positive possibilities of change
4 Looks outside the operation for ideas and new ways of thinking
5 Constantly seeks to improve the way that things are done
6 Encourages others to develop new ideas
7 Uses brainstorming and other creative techniques
8 Challenges the fixed thinking of others
9 Treats mistakes as opportunities for learning
10 Celebrates successes

**2 ♥ Lover** (see p. 108)

1 Actively builds and maintains relationships
2 Communicates openly
3 Really listens to others
4 Operates practices based on trust
5 Gives praise when it is due
6 Acts to reduce stress in the organisation
7 Encourages others to learn
8 Takes time out to guide and develop others
9 Is an effective coach and mentor
10 Is both honest and fair

**3 ➵ Warrior** (see p. 108)

1 Inspires confidence in the possibilities of the future
2 Acts with confidence in public
3 Agrees demanding targets
4 Makes timely decisions and communicates them clearly
5 Is willing to take difficult decisions
6 Will defend individuals and teams from internal and external threats
7 Deals quickly with underperformance
8 Influences and persuades upwards, downwards and sideways
9 Thrives on challenges
10 Achieves outstanding results

| 4 ♕ **Sovereign** (see p. 108) |
| --- |
| 1 Sets clear direction and strategies |
| 2 Creates and communicates a set of values |
| 3 Is politically intelligent and able to read situations |
| 4 Is personally well organised |
| 5 Delegates clearly and effectively |
| 6 Considers ethical issues before making decisions |
| 7 Can deal effectively with the needs of different stakeholders |
| 8 Keeps promises |
| 9 Is calm in a crisis |
| 10 Is both just and merciful |

*Example is not the main thing in influencing others. It is the only thing.*

Albert Schweitzer, Nobel Prize winner

→ Match your own skills with the leadership job requirement.

→ Get some feedback on your own leadership performance.

→ Recognise where you need to improve and plan to do something about it.

→ Constantly evaluate everything you do against the leadership requirements.

→ Others judge you every day – why not judge yourself?

## Read around

*Inspirational leadership*, R. Olivier

## Links to other leadership tips

**Chapter 6** Recognising that people are different and motivating them differently

**18** Decide your own set of values

**19** Use the set of values that you have created

**20** Reconcile personal values when they don't align with organisational behaviours

**21** Tell when it is time to resign

**23** Keep your promises

**24** Create a set of team or organisational values

**25** Embed new behaviours in line with the values in your organisation

**42** Undertake your own self-development

**43** Write and implement your own leadership development plan

# Leadership tip **23**

# Keep your PROMISES

*A business plan is
a promise to deliver.*

Bill Stanway, former
Chief Executive, ITT,
London and Edinburgh

One of the good things about being in charge is that you, as the leader, are the one who chooses the level of expectation that other people develop about your operation. This is a function of both the level of your promises to deliver and your ability to deliver on your promises.

### Use your values

Before you make a promise to deliver ask yourself whether this promise is in line with your values.

In addition:

**1 Allow for the unexpected** – no matter how confident you are in your own abilities and those of your team, remember Murphy's Law that states, 'If something can go wrong, it will'. Include some allowance in your promises for the unexpected.

**2 Nothing is idiot proof** – although you may have laboured long and hard to put together a winning team, you will always come across someone who is bent on making your life as a leader difficult. If you haven't allowed for this possibility, you are asking for trouble.

**3 Under-promising and over-delivering** – one strategy to keep out of harm's way is to under-promise and maximise the chances that you can beat the target. If your boss wants 15% growth, you can fight hard to reduce the target to 10%, knowing that you are likely to come in at 12%. This way you are not a hero but you probably still have your job.

**4 Over-promising and under-delivering** – the far more dangerous strategy is not to deliver what you have promised. Making promises at the drop of a hat is careless. Unless you are absolutely certain that you can deliver on a promise, don't make it. Find other words, such as 'I think we may be able to do that by the end of the month' or 'There's only a reasonable chance of us being able to do that ...'. Then lay out the conditions.

**5 Put and get promises in writing** – aside from covering your behind, writing things down is the best way of clarifying what you actually propose to do. Make sure that you put deadlines and milestones in your diary and that you brief everyone concerned about what you have promised.

Source: adapted from M. Loeb and S. Kindel, *Leadership for dummies*

## In practice...

*In the late 1980s Brian worked as the marketing director for a firm of insurance brokers. The firm had a new product that he decided to publicise by holding a conference. In those days the attitude of his peer group of managers was that insurance brokers did not organise conferences and he received little internal support.*

*In a rash moment he got his own marketing staff together and promised them that if they managed to get together a paying audience of 200 for the event, he would treat them all to dinner at the Savoy – one of the best hotels in London.*

*His staff achieved the objective. The conference title was topical, the venue was excellent and the pricing right. Within a week of the mailshot going out, places were sold out.*

*Brian honoured his promise. Soon afterwards the staff of the marketing department dined at the Savoy.*

## Read around

Leadership for dummies, M. Loeb and S. Kindel

## Links to other leadership tips

**18** Decide your own set of values

**19** Use the set of values that you have created

**20** Reconcile personal values when they don't align with organisational behaviours

**21** Tell when it is time to resign

**22** Set a good example

**24** Create a set of team or organisational values

**25** Embed new behaviours in line with the values in your organisation

# Create a set of TEAM OR ORGANISATIONAL VALUES

A set of values that will determine the way we do business cannot be mandated from the top. Everyone involved must be included in the determination process and encouraged to have their say.

Hold a workshop with the purpose of creating a set of agreed values and make sure that everyone is briefed beforehand.

| Values workshop |
| --- |
| **1** Explain the concept of a set of values. |
| **2** Give examples of personal and team or organisational values. The list of possible values on page 85 may be of use here. |
| **3** State that the list must be short – between three and five words. |
| **4** If necessary split people into work-sized groups of five to seven. |
| **5** Set the task of coming up with an agreed set of values. Encourage the use of brainstorming or other creative techniques. |
| **6** Have enough dictionaries present and encourage their use. |
| **7** Ask team leaders to present their set of recommended values and explain what it means in the context of the organisation. |
| **8** Ask questions such as what this value implies about the way that we make decisions, the way that we conduct meetings; what does this mean for our client base, our appraisal system, etc. |
| **9** Arrive at an agreed list and publish to all concerned. |

## In practice...

*The rugby World Cup-winning England squad adopted a set of values that was incorporated in its teamship rules.*

*Among them was a commitment to ensuring that no one in the squad should appear in a bad light in any book or newspaper column written by a squad member: no player, no coach, no doctor – nobody.*

### Read around

*Winning,* Sir Clive Woodward

### Links to other leadership tips

# EMBED NEW BEHAVIOURS in line with the values in your organisation

Many change programmes fail because leaders do not take action to reward the new behaviours. Instead they continue to reward the achievement of task-related outcomes, whether or not the ends are achieved in an acceptable way. For example the salesman who meets his target but does not follow through with timely information to customer support, or the manager who continues to work and expect long hours when the organisation has decided to implement family-friendly approaches.

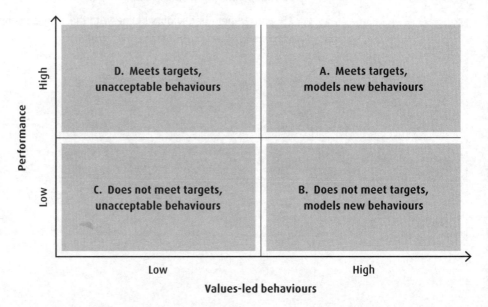

**A. Meets targets, models new behaviours** – these are your stars, promote them quickly. This will send a powerful message to the organisation that you are serious about the change.

**B. Does not meet targets, models new behaviours** – these are candidates for coaching. They need encouragement to improve performance while maintaining the new behaviours.

**C. Does not meet targets, unacceptable behaviours** – sack these people.

**D. Meets targets, unacceptable behaviours** – these are the most dangerous group of people. It is essential to tackle their failure to change. Use the 'three strikes and you're out' rule. Be clear that behaviour and task targets are equally important, point out the failure on behaviours, agree the changed behaviour needed and if it is not achieved in three review stages, sack them. Not doing this will virtually guarantee the failure of your change programme.

## In practice...

*General Electric put all expected values-driven behaviours for each role openly on its intranet. Within 12 months the values were embedded – those who saw them as a threat left.*

## Read around

*Making six sigma last*, G. Eckes

## Links to other leadership tips

18  Decide your own set of values

19  Use the set of values that you have created

20  Reconcile personal values when they don't align with organisational behaviours

21  Tell when it is time to resign

22  Set a good example

23  Keep your promises

24  Create a set of team or organisational values

# Chapter 6
# Recognising that people are different and motivating them differently

STEP 1
Thinking like a leader

STEP 2
Creating a vision

STEP 3
Choosing a set of values

STEP 4
Recognising that people are different

STEP 5
Achieving extraordinary results

# Leadership tip **26**

# Use DISTINCTION-BASED learning

*Two men look through
the same bars;
one sees mud and
the other stars.*

Frank Langbridge,
author

A distinction is a way of organising what we see, hear or feel. The different ways we experience the world is a function of the distinctions we are able to draw. One child on the beach runs away in terror from a large wave. Another child's eyes light up with excitement as she jumps to let it wash over her. It's the same wave. The two children just view it differently.

The more distinctions we can draw the more powerful our analysis of any experience can become. It is said that the Zulus have 39 words for describing the green of the forest. The more distinctions about their natural habitat that they can draw, the more comfortable they can make their lives.

### In practice...

*Statistically yellow-painted Volkswagen cars are scarce. However, if you suspect your partner of having an affair with someone who drives a yellow Volkswagen, you will start to notice them every-where. What is scarce has become common through distinguishing powerfully.*

Useful distinctions to draw as a leader are:

→ To separate the person from their action. Just because a member of your team makes one bad mistake does not make them a bad employee. You can distinguish the sinner from the sin – forgiving the sinner but not the sin.

→ You can apply the same thinking to your own actions as a leader. One failure does not make you a bad leader – it is just an experience from which you can learn to improve in the future.

→ You can distinguish powerfully by recognising that people are different. They have different ways of thinking, acting and being. A good leader knows that people have to be motivated in different ways.

Distinction-based learning is not a quick-fix solution. You have to work at making distinctions. You cannot become a cricket buff, a wine connoisseur or a successful leader overnight. You even have to work at spotting yellow Volkswagens. It's the same when learning to distinguish between the differences in people. It is a skill that needs practice.

### Read around

*The last word on power,* T. Goss

### Links to other leadership tips

## Leadership tip **27**

# Value the DIFFERENCES IN PEOPLE

Almost all leaders would agree that they experience different responses to their ideas or proposals from different people. Occasionally an idea is well received; sometimes the same idea proposed to someone else meets with a negative response.

Every human being is shaped by innumerable influences. These can include gender, race, parental values, religion, profession, education, area of upbringing as well as the genes we inherited; and these are all mixed up with our own individual personality and preferences. Every human being is unique and has a unique way of viewing the world.

→ Valuing the differences in people is to understand fully that the way we see our world is not the way others see their world. Recognising that the different ways in which others see their world can add to our own knowledge and understanding of concepts, problems and challenges.

→ Accept that we need to put aside our selfish need to 'be right', to suspend our judgement and encourage a view that there can, paradoxically, be several correct solutions to every problem that life throws at us.

→ Think of conversation as a dialogue rather than a debate. Ask and encourage others to explain the way that they see things. Use open questions that do not try to get just the answer you want. Listen first to understand and only then seek to be understood.

→ Inquire into the assumptions you are making about the situation or the persons involved. Make a list of these assumptions and be open about them.

→ Allow time for your own reflection on situations. Think about things and, if it helps, write them down. Write about feelings as well as facts.

→ In conversation try to 'go with the flow' rather than arguing every point. Use 'Yes and…' as opposed to 'Yes but…' Try to see connections and possibilities rather than objections.

→ Speak up for what you really believe to be right after you have thought through the situation and your own reaction to it.

*No snowflake ever falls in the wrong place.*

Zen saying

## In practice...

*The first time Roger went to work in the USA he was amazed at what he perceived to be the 'greed' of the American staff in his office. The first topic of conversation every morning seemed to centre on the financial growth of their stock options. Roger, brought up in the world of work in the UK, was used to the concept of an annual bonus in stock options following outstanding performance. In the USA at that time a stated bonus seemed to be the expectation for norm performance. It was almost as though the bonus came before the performance.*

*It was not until Roger learned that Americans do not have the same pension rights as their equivalents in the UK that he understood their need to 'make a pile' whilst at work to avoid poverty in retirement. He recognised that the different national contexts were driving different attitudes and behaviours, yet the values, providing for the family, were exactly the same.*

## Read around

*Dialogue*, L. Ellinor and G. Gerrard

*The X & Y of leadership*, L. Cook and B. Rothwell

## Links to other leadership tips

**26** Use distinction-based learning

**28** Recognise the differences in people

**41** Recognise and use the difference between debate and dialogue

**48** Get into that state of ultra-high performance known as flow

# Leadership tip **28**

# Recognise the DIFFERENCES IN PEOPLE

**A universal model**

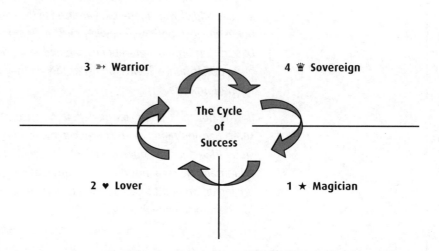

Everything in life starts in the place of the magician with a little piece of magic. A new project starts with the spark of an idea, a seed starts to germinate when it meets fertile soil and water, or a child is conceived.

It then proceeds to the place of the lover, where the idea is nurtured and given tender loving care. It is necessary for people to get used to any new idea. A plant is fertilised, pruned and cared for. A child is loved and made to feel safe.

Once nurtured, the idea must go out into the real world and compete for resources, for budget or for space in crowded schedules. This is the place of the warrior. A plant has to compete for light and water in a crowded garden or field. A child must go to school and compete both inside and outside the classroom.

If the competing goes well, then the project must be systematised and rules applied to its continuing existence. This is the place of the sovereign. The plant produces its fruit or its flowers which are systematically cut. A child grows and recognises the need for rules and regulations to keep society safe.

And once organised we must then proceed around the figure and embrace the prospect of another new idea in the place of the magician. The model is in continual flow.

*There are three things that are extremely hard: steel, a diamond and to know oneself.*

Benjamin Franklin, former US President

Without this concentration on all four areas companies and organisations die. They may die slowly but they die.

Source: model adapted from G. Hill, *Masculine and feminine*

### *In practice...*

*In the 1980s the computer giant IBM became, as an organisation, stuck in the place of the Sovereign. They were preoccupied with their own internal processes and their assumptions about how the market for computers would develop. They did not believe that individual PCs would be the way of the future and ignored the potential of that development.*

*At the same time Bill Gates, CEO Microsoft, who was operating in the place of the magician, was busy developing Windows and associated Microsoft products, all of which were aimed at the personal computer market.*

*IBM had forgotten the need to revisit the place of the magician in order to challenge current thinking and develop ideas for new product ranges.*

*Microsoft is now bigger than IBM.*

### *Read around*

*Inspirational leadership,* R. Olivier

*Masculine and feminine, the natural flows of opposites in the psyche,* G. Hill

### *Links to other leadership tips*

**29** Apply the universal model to leadership

**30** Recognise and motivate a magician

**31** Recognise and motivate a lover

**32** Recognise and motivate a warrior

**33** Recognise and motivate a sovereign

**34** Use the universal model to evaluate your team, your key stakeholders or anyone else.

# Apply the UNIVERSAL MODEL to leadership

Most of us would accept that people are different. We think differently and act in different ways when faced with the same stimuli. However, as leaders at work it is helpful to have a convenient way of grouping differences together. And the groupings must be few enough to be usable by busy individuals under pressure.

*The purpose of models is not to fit the data, but to sharpen the questions.*

Samuel Karlin

The universal model can be applied to people. All individuals have preferred ways of thinking, acting and being. Some are better warriors; others are better lovers; yet others are better magicians and still others better sovereigns. Each of us has at least one preferred quadrant – many of us have a blend of two quadrants and some of us a blend of three. However, only the saints and Maria Theresa could claim to excel in all four areas.

It is our contention that the most commonly used psychometric materials used at work today have too many personality types for the busy line manager at work to remember. Myers Briggs has sixteen and Belbin has nine. They all spring from the same source – the Jungian four psychological archetypes. We have boiled everything down to these four types because we have proved to our own satisfaction that ordinary individuals who are not specialists in the subject can remember our four personality archetypes.

As with all generalisations, these ideas should not be taken as rigid frameworks, always 100% true. Think of them as metaphors, generally applicable and as an aid to reflection – a starting point for your own ideas. They provide a fun and non-threatening language for people to discuss and understand their differences.

The sources and links to other psychometric materials are shown opposite.

| The Myers Briggs personality types* | |
|---|---|
| **NT** iNtuitive Thinking | **ST** Sensing Thinking |
| – **ENTJ** Extroverted iNtuitive Thinking Judging | – **ESTJ** Extroverted Sensing Thinking Judging |
| – **INTJ** Introverted iNtuitive Thinking Judging | – **ISTJ** Introverted Sensing Thinking Judging |
| – **ENTP** Extroverted iNtuitive Thinking Perceiving | – **ESTP** Extroverted Sensing Thinking Perceiving |
| – **INTP** Introverted iNtuitive Thinking Perceiving | – **ISTP** Introverted Sensing Thinking Perceiving |
| **NF** iNtuitive Feeling | **SF** Sensing Feeling |
| – **ENFJ** Extroverted iNtuitive Feeling Judging | – **ESFJ** Extroverted Sensing Feeling Judging |
| – **INFJ** Introverted iNtuitive Feeling Judging | – **ISFJ** Introverted Sensing Feeling Judging |
| – **ENFP** Extroverted iNtuitive Feeling Perceiving | – **ESFP** Extroverted Sensing Feeling Perceiving |
| – **INFP** Introverted iNtuitive Feeling Perceiving | – **ISFP** Introverted Sensing Feeling Perceiving |

| | Myers Briggs types* | Maslow Hierarchy of needs | Belbin Team roles | Sante Fe Pyramid of conversation | Kolb Learning styles |
|---|---|---|---|---|---|
| ⚐ **Warrior** | NT<br><br>– ENTJ<br>– INTJ<br>– ENTP<br>– INTP | Physiological Basic<br><br>Fear of extinction | Shaper | Conversation for action | Activist |
| ♛ **Sovereign** | ST<br><br>– ESTJ<br>– ISTJ<br>– ESTP<br>– ISTP | Security and order<br><br>Fear of Chaos | Completer-finisher<br><br>Monitor-evaluator<br><br>Chairman<br><br>Company worker | Conversation for opportunity | Reflector |
| ★ **Magician** | NF<br><br>– ENFJ<br>– INFJ<br>– ENFP<br>– INFP | Self-identity<br><br>Fear of loss of self-identity | Plant<br><br>Resource investigator | Conversation for possibility | Theorist |
| ♥ **Lover** | SF<br><br>– ESFJ<br>– ISFJ<br>– ESFP<br>– ISFP | Belonging<br><br>Fear of rejection | Team worker | Conversation for relationship | Pragmatist |

Leaders need to know their strong and weak suits. They also need to know that their strong suit has a shadow side. For example a strong magician may want too much change in the department and by so doing, de-motivate some staff. A strong sovereign may want things run by the book and produce a similar demotivation.

If you wish to know your own strongest and weakest areas, please refer to the questionnaire in the Appendix.

Every leader needs to know that their people are all different and that different people need to be handled differently. A lover needs different treatment than a warrior to perform well. If the leader is a sovereign she cannot expect all others to respond well to her need for analysis and taking careful decisions using data.

Because teams and even organisations usually follow the behavioural example of those they admire they can also exhibit group behaviour as one of the four archetypes.

### How we tend to view each other

Awareness starts with 'knowing thyself' and your leadership strengths and potential weaknesses. The second step is to have respect for individuals and teams who are different. The final step is to be able to communicate in such different ways that every individual has the confidence to give of their best.

So if a leader is making a speech or writing a report for general consumption, consideration must be given to appealing to each of the four archetypes irrespective of the leader's strongest suit. Only in this way will she or he appeal to all.

We all start in our dominant quadrant and we view each other both positively and negatively from that point of view.

The following pages outline the main characteristics of each of the four archetypes.

### In practice...

*A sales team and their telesales support were trained to recognise the four types of customers and change their responses accordingly. In the first year their combined sales increased 25%.*

## Read around

*Experiential learning,* D. Kolb

*People types and tiger stripes,* G. Lawrence

*Management teams, why they succeed or fail,* M. Belbin

*Type talk at work,* O. Kroeger and J.M. Thuesen

## Links to other leadership tips

# Leadership tip **30**

# Recognise and motivate a MAGICIAN

Magicians have a 'visionary' mentality and they see life as a journey. They see everyone and everything in a process of change. Magicians like gadgets; they wear bright, unusual clothes and drive quirky cars. They are a tad eccentric and big into interior design of their homes. They read fantasy novels and science fiction. Many of them can be found in careers like graphic designing.

Magicians have considerable strengths. They:

→ Possess a dominant right brain and focus on the future.

→ Need to look ahead, to consider new options and to promote change.

→ Have an ability to see the big picture, new patterns and new possibilities, and they learn by visualising the end results.

→ Value and enjoy non-routine work, imagination, newness.

→ Delegate a lot but they may leave the delegatee alone and sometimes forget to whom they delegated.

→ Like a brainstorming style of teaching. 'Let's run this one up the flagpole'; 'Let's see if this one will fly.'

→ Have a tendency to speak mystically about visions, theories and concepts. Often they will repeat their views.

→ Like to be seen as a person with original and different thoughts.

→ Freely express opinions with complex and expansive viewpoints. They take a lot of time for talking but may be poor listeners.

→ Can identify lots of problems ahead and may have a pessimistic tendency.

→ Seek novel and original products, services and experiences.

→ Desire to have their own identity in a team as an ideas person and be free to hold and express views.

→ Need time to dream and therefore fear acting in haste without considering all the options. They also fear a loss of individual freedom of thought and expression.

A magician can be viewed negatively by others because of the impact of these preferences. A warrior may think that this individual is all talk with a head that is in the clouds, rather too impractical and unrealistic, too theoretical or conceptual, a bit of a weirdo or an anorak. A sovereign may think him or her a dreamer and too futuristic, irrational and undisciplined, always seeing obstacles and ignoring facts and data. A lover may see a magician as too change orientated, unconcerned about continuity and with no sense of loyalty.

However the reverse is also true; others could see a magician as:

→ coming up with ideas;

→ a see-er of the big picture;

→ relating well to theory;

→ imaginative;

→ unafraid to stand alone;

→ a see-er of the need for change;

→ not tied to old ways;

→ not put off by the fears of others;

→ far seeing.

## In practice...

*Steve's strongest suit is that of the magician. He has previously worked as a reinsurance broker and on the sales side for a charity. Significantly, he now works for himself.*

*He comments 'If you want to get the best out of me give me a free rein, don't tie me down with job descriptions and targets. Let me explore new areas for business and different connections. I am an ideas person.'*

### How to build rapport with a magician

Relate to change, what is new and the big picture.

### Do:

→ Give magicians freedom of thought, expression, movement and how they use their time.

→ Give them what they want but on your terms. They do not want a standard package of anything – job contract, room layout, computer, car etc. They want newness, change and originality. They want lean lines, compactness and style.

*Life is painting
a picture not
doing a sum.*

Oliver Wendell
Holmes, author, jurist

→ Develop a big picture and focus on the long-term future. Say 'Imagine what our organisation could be in three years' time…' Give them big boundaries and lots of space.

→ Ask them if you want something written or designed.

→ Ask them if you are in need of new ideas; they will have hundreds.

→ Let them do what they are good at. They are terrific at brainstorming and other creative techniques.

→ Say 'My time is your time' and then listen to them. Use your listening skills and have patience.

→ Be prepared to listen to a wide-ranging discussion covering diverse subjects and opinions.

→ Be interested for the sake of interest.

→ Show pictures, sketches; let them draw.

→ Express appreciation in terms they like to hear. Remember they like to think they are original thinkers and possess unique gadgets.

→ Expect a cautious, conceptual decision-making approach even though they have hundreds of ideas

→ Do say 'If we can provide you with this … and this … and this … would you agree?'.

→ Beware of the impracticality of many of their ideas.

**Do not:**

→ Appear to have all of the answers.

→ Restrict them by using tight managerial controls.

→ Try to get them to do detailed routine work.

→ Say 'This is what has worked well elsewhere'.

→ Push them for a quick decision.

→ Mention that this is the most popular approach to solving this problem.

→ Speak of your own hobby horses and interests; they have enough of their own.

→ Try to make the conversation practical. Magicians are not concerned about details like price, cost, time to completion or delivery times.

## Read around

*Inspirational leadership*, R. Olivier

*Peak performance presentations*, R. Olivier and N. Janni

## Links to other leadership tips

**28** Recognise the differences in people

**29** Apply the universal model to leadership

**31** Recognise and motivate a lover

**32** Recognise and motivate a warrior

**33** Recognise and motivate a sovereign

**34** Use the universal model to evaluate your team, your key stakeholders or anyone else

# Leadership tip **31**
# Recognise and motivate a LOVER

*Whoever is happy will make others happy too.*

Anne Frank, teenage author, war victim

Lovers have a 'martyr' mentality in that they see everything and everyone as needing their help. They have a community view of the world – 'Life and work is for the benefit of all'.

They have photographs of friends and family prominently on display in their homes and offices. Their homes have a lived-in feel. Their door is always open and they talk a lot especially on the phone. Above all they put others before themselves. Many of them can be found in careers in the caring professions.

Lovers have considerable strengths. They:

→ Possess a dominant right brain and their time focus is on the past.

→ Value and enjoy the company of others, teamwork and loyalty.

→ Value relationships and therefore fear being hurt, let down or rejected by others.

→ Seek to 'fit in' and achieve consensus.

→ Are concerned about emotions and people issues.

→ Have a desire to belong, for informality, harmony and friendliness.

→ Like to feel valued and appreciated and accepted as an important team member.

→ Learn by consulting, exchanging views with others, preferably face to face.

→ Need a counselling style of teaching – 'How does that feel?'; 'On a scale 1–10 would this be beneficial?'.

→ Speak in warm tones – 'touchy-feely' and caring.

→ Are very good at identifying the people problems in all change initiatives.

→ Need continuity and a relationship between the past and present.

→ Give opinions with emotion, but with concern not to offend or distance others.

→ Seek experience of others when making buying decisions; they use referrals and need friendly assurance.

→ Need to trust you to work with you and, as a result, if you betray that trust they can be judgemental and hold grudges.

118

A lover can be viewed negatively by others. A warrior could think a lover too easily upset, too concerned about others, a ditherer who is slow to act with a negative attitude, a bit of a wimp. A sovereign might think that he or she is too emotional, non-rational and logical, makes mountains out of molehills, a nosey meddler in the affairs of others. A magician may find a lover too tradition bound, stuck in a rut, too tied to social rules, resistant to change or afraid to upset others.

Again the reverse is true; others could see a lover as:

→ sensitive to key issues;

→ a see-er of good in others;

→ cautious to offend;

→ caring;

→ an intuitive reasoner;

→ good at people issues;

→ good at relationships;

→ a valuer of important traditions;

→ concerned for those in need.

### *In practice...*

*Jenny's strongest suit is that of the lover. She works for a property company making sure that reception areas and common parts of office suites are furnished and decorated to standard.*

*She comments: 'If you want to get the best out of me spend time to build a relationship with me. I work best for those I trust and for those whose values I respect. I like friendly meetings and decisions that are made by consensus'.*

### How to build rapport with a lover

Build trust, resolve emotive issues and talk about people. Lovers want a relationship.

### Do:

→ Be personable, informal and friendly. Above all, smile.

→ Tell them about your family, holiday, weekend etc.
   They are really interested.

> *It doesn't take much to keep me happy; just a phone call and a little appreciation of my needs.*
>
> Ann Paul, executive, voluntary sector

→ Develop a conversation; make a friend. Talk to them about themselves.

→ Ask their opinion, take their opinions seriously.

→ Remember birthdays and anniversaries.

→ Empathise with their predicament.

→ Use emotive words like 'feel', 'felt' and 'found'. Lovers are concerned about feelings.

→ Work to gain their trust; lovers buy *you* rather than a result or an outcome.

→ Emphasise people issues and concerns. Lovers are concerned about people.

→ Be patient; lovers need your time.

→ Focus on the relationship for the sake of the relationship, not on what you want out of the relationship.

→ Lovers need to know what has worked elsewhere; they need reference points and testimonials. Take them to see the proposed solution in action and let them talk to the people on site.

→ Let them focus on details like colour, design and layout.

→ Adopt a caring, consensus decision-making approach.

**Do not:**

→ Be big, boisterous and loudly enthusiastic.

→ Rush them.

→ Ask them to work on a project alone.

→ Show them that you are impatient.

→ Push them for a quick decision.

→ Criticise what appears to you to be a slow decision-making process.

→ Focus on a cost-benefit analysis or other detailed processes.

→ Use 'blue sky' techniques or brainstorming.

→ Get angry.

## Read around

*Inspirational leadership*, R. Olivier

*Peak performance presentations*, R. Olivier and N. Janni

## Links to other leadership tips

**28** Recognise the differences in people

**29** Apply the universal model to leadership

**30** Recognise and motivate a magician

**32** Recognise and motivate a warrior

**33** Recognise and motivate a sovereign

**34** Use the universal model to evaluate your team, your key stakeholders or anyone else

# Leadership tip **32**

# **Recognise and motivate a WARRIOR**

*Just do it.*

Nike advertising slogan

Warriors are optimistic and action orientated. They have a 'hammer' mentality in the extreme they see everything and everyone as a 'nail' or another tool. They drive utilitarian cars that are usually dirty from carting around DIY materials. A grubby seven-year-old four-wheel-drive is a good clue to the owner being a warrior. They are big into competitive sports. They are direct, opinionated and confrontational. They compete in conversation to tell the best joke or the best story. Many can be found in careers that involve doing, building or competing for things.

Warriors have considerable strengths. They:

→ Possess a dominant left brain and their time focus is on the here and now.

→ Have a need for movement and action to respond to a situation. They see being busy as doing things – taking action to 'make things happen'.

→ Fear acting too slowly and have no time for thinking, dreaming or dwelling on issues.

→ Learn by doing. They value and enjoy physical and practical activities – DIY, walking, skiing, sailing.

→ Have a self-oriented view of the world – 'I need'; 'I want'; 'I'.

→ Prefer to be in charge – they have a desire to control surroundings and people.

→ Make decisions subjectively and impulsively and as a result they may need to think more laterally before acting.

→ Need a directive, tell-like teaching style – 'Do this'; 'Move it'; 'Get on with it'; 'Do it my way'.

→ Speak their minds, get straight to the point, call 'a spade a spade' – there is no waffle

→ Must be confronted because they are demanding, confrontational, stubborn and respect strength of mind. 'When I want your opinion I'll ask for it.' May need to attend charm school. They are poor listeners.

→ Seek practical value, uses and discounts when buying – they are hard negotiators.

A warrior can be viewed negatively by other archetypes. A sovereign may think a warrior impulsive, a poor analyser, a messy worker, a trial-and-error merchant, all rush and no finesse, an uncouth yobbo. A lover could see him or her as uncaring, self-centred and bossy, a poor listener with no time and always in a hurry, impolite and brusque, a bit of a dictator. A magician can view a warrior as a 'have-a-go' merchant, simple minded, a short term-ist, an all-rush action man, a control freak, a bit of a dim wit.

A warrior could however be seen positively by others as:

→ good in an emergency;

→ unafraid to try things;

→ a quick fixer;

→ prepared to get his or her hands dirty;

→ an ignorer of others' complaints;

→ someone who gets to the point;

→ a strong arm when needed;

→ a see-er of immediate problems;

→ a cutter-out of crap.

### *In practice...*

*Mark is a warrior. He has worked in sales management and business development for an insurance company for more than 30 years.*

*He comments: 'I have always been competitive, both at work and on the golf course. If you want to get the best out of me, set me a target and watch me beat it. Don't burden me with too many meetings, let me get out there and make the sale. I like to win, there are no prizes for coming second – are there?'.*

**How to develop rapport with a warrior. Get to the point, be practical. Warriors want a result.**

**Do:**

→ Set them targets; they like to win.

→ Construct competitive situations; they like to compete with each other. However, do not let them compete with other personality types.

- → Give them something to be in charge of, even if it's only the stationery store cupboard – warriors like to be in charge.
- → Involve them if you want something started with enthusiasm: they can motivate and do pep talks.
- → Appeal to their pride.
- → Recognise their achievements in private, but, even better, in public.
- → Keep meetings short and to the point.
- → Use an agenda and times and stick to them.
- → Be positive.
- → Emphasise practical, functional and cost-effective benefits.
- → Aim to make things happen and happen quickly.
- → Be assertive, expect to be challenged.
- → Be prepared to negotiate; warriors like to negotiate.
- → Focus on the short term and practical next steps.
- → Push for a quick decision.
- → Expect decisiveness from them and agreement to action.
- → Confront them if you disagree.

**Do not:**

- → Tell them details of your family, holiday, etc. They are not interested.
- → Be nosey. Warriors don't talk about their own personal details.
- → Use emotional heaviness. They just can't cope with it.
- → Theorise or intellectualise.
- → Keep them waiting.
- → Keep talking if you can see that they are ready for action.
- → Go to them for sympathy or comfort; you won't get any.
- → Expect subtlety; they are incapable of it.

## Read around

*Inspirational leadership*, R. Olivier

*Peak performance presentations*, R. Olivier and N. Janni

## Links to other leadership tips

# Leadership tip **33**

# **Recognise and motivate a SOVEREIGN**

*A place for everything and everything in its place.*

Proverb

Sovereigns posses a 'computer' mentality and in the extreme see everyone and everything as a quantifiable asset or liability. They drive spotless, value for money cars that they have purchased after reading *Which* magazine. They have gardens with lawns that have knife-edges and the hose is neatly coiled. They only have one file out on the desk at a time. Status conscious, their name and title may be on the office door or desk. Many can be found in careers like accountancy or librarianship.

Sovereigns have considerable strengths. They:

→ Possess a dominant left brain and their time focus is on the immediate past.

→ Need to collect facts and data and they like to think and plan before acting.

→ Fear acting in error and therefore dislike not having time to collect and check facts upon which decisions depend.

→ Learn by reading, analysing and referring to documents.

→ Value and enjoy work requiring exacting, precise analysis within a procedural framework.

→ Have an organised view of the world. Life is a diary of appointments.

→ Have a decision-making style that needs to analyse and 'think before you act'. Factual evidence is key.

→ Have a desire for structure, formality, standard routines, systems, clear roles and order. They regard rules as sacrosanct. 'A rule is a rule.'

→ Need a direct coaching style of teaching – 'Try this'; Take this approach'; 'I suggest …'.

→ Are neat and tidy.

→ Speak about facts, data and figures rather than feelings.

→ Like things in writing and logically presented.

→ Give opinions when asked. They have attended charm school and are good listeners.

→ Make buying decisions by seeking value for money and checking out all prices and specifications.

Others can view sovereigns negatively. A warrior may think a sovereign slow and indecisive – afraid to act quickly, status orientated, a rule-bound administrator, a tedious nitpicker. A lover may view a sovereign as condescending, overly formal, cold, robotic and clinical, logical and uncaring, an uninteresting bore, a bit of a snob. A magician can view a sovereign as having no imagination, narrow minded, concerned only with facts and data, a supporter of the status quo, a bean counter.

However, others could see a sovereign as:

→ good with facts and data;

→ a bringer of order;

→ a tidy mind;

→ a clinical and logical thinker;

→ someone who makes you pause and think;

→ a see-er of flaws;

→ good with formalities;

→ a developer of procedures;

→ a recogniser of specialisms.

### *In practice...*

*Jo is a sovereign. She is an accountant and has practised her profession for more than 20 years. She comments: 'I like to take all my decisions both at work and at home carefully after researching all of the avenues available. I would never buy a car without consulting* Which? *magazine and* Dalton's Weekly. *If you want to get the best out of me, give me time and don't rush me. Above all don't make me work in an untidy environment.'*

### How to build rapport with a sovereign

Present and build a logical case, put things in writing. Sovereigns want value for money; their rhythm is conciseness.

### Do:

→ Be deferential, formal, smart and polite.

→ Use titles and Mr, Ms, Mrs, Dr, etc. and make sure you get them right.

*The journey of a thousand miles starts with a single step.*

Chinese proverb

→ Call them if you need a project seen through to the end and done right.

→ Be on time, agree how much time is needed and finish on time.

→ Invite them in if you need the qualities of patience, practicality and persistence.

→ Use their reliability and stability.

→ Adopt an unemotional and positive outlook.

→ Go through everything in detail from the bottom up; provide plans, specifications, facts and procedures.

→ Let them prepare their checklists and spreadsheets; this is the way sovereigns work things out.

→ Use statistical techniques and cost-benefit analyses.

→ Be detailed and explain everything.

→ Quantify as much as you can.

→ Expect a logical, rational decision-making process.

→ Put as much in writing as possible.

**Do not:**

→ Waffle.

→ Push them for a quick decision; they need to have studied the details.

→ Expect spontaneity or flexibility.

→ Ask them to 'blue sky'; remember they work from the bottom up.

→ Expect them to enjoy the limelight; they need private not public recognition.

→ Theorise.

→ Expect them to be sensitive and show their emotions.

→ Answer one of their questions with a question. If you don't know, tell them that you don't know and when you will have the answer.

→ Put your brief case on their desk.

### Read around

*Inspirational leadership*, R. Olivier

*Peak performance presentations*, R. Olivier and N. Janni

### Links to other leadership tips

## Leadership tip **34**

# Use the universal model to evaluate your TEAM, your key stakeholders or anyone else

If you have not already done so, please read leadership tips 30–33 on the previous pages, which will remind you of the main characteristics of the four archetypes.

Most people would regard Margaret Thatcher and Ian Botham as primarily being warriors and Princess Diana and Terry Wogan as lovers. Most would also identify Mr Spock from Star Trek and Sir Humphry Appleby from the 'Yes Minister' TV series as primarily being sovereigns, and entrepreneurs Richard Branson and Richard Dyson as magicians.

**Your team's personality archetypes**

Have a go at identifying the primary types of the individuals who work most closely with you. Create a chart like the example below to record your initial judgements.

|  | ★ Magician | ♥ Lover | ⇒ Warrior | ♛ Sovereign |
|---|---|---|---|---|
| Alena | ✔ |  |  |  |
| Boris |  |  |  | ✔ |
| Colin |  | ✔ |  |  |
| Dana |  |  | ✔ |  |
| Etc. |  |  |  |  |

Bear in mind that the best teams are those in which all four types are represented. If you find a gap or a serious imbalance try to recruit individuals to fill the gaps. Failing that, and it may not always be possible to expand the team in this way, you as leader need to pay attention to the missing aspects and ensure that the team takes enough time and recognises the importance of the thinking that is lacking in its discussions.

> *We hold these truths to be self evident that all men are created equal.*
>
> Thomas Jefferson, third US President

## Read around

*Inspirational leadership*, R. Olivier

*Peak performance presentations*, R. Olivier and N. Janni

## Links to other leadership tips

# Chapter 7
# Achieving extraordinary results as an individual leader

**STEP 1**
Thinking like a leader

**STEP 2**
Creating a vision

**STEP 3**
Choosing a set of values

**STEP 4**
Recognising that people are different

**STEP 5**
Achieving extraordinary results

# Leadership tip **35**
# ANALYSE problems

The left hemisphere of the brain is devoted to logical analysis, cause and effect and linear progressions. This type of thinking is fairly familiar in Western civilisations and is the basis of standard computer logic – begin at the beginning, 'If A then B', and so on. However when faced with problems at work it can sometimes de difficult to decide where to begin and even, on occasion, when you have reached the end. Developing a **logical** approach to problems will give you greater confidence in your ability to find solutions to them.

The key steps are to understand the:

> **Level,**
>
> **Operational impact** and
>
> **Givens of the problem.**

Use your **Instinct,**

be **Creative,**

take **Action** and ensure that your organisation

**Learns** from the experience.

*Always look at the whole of a thing. Find what it is that makes an impression on you. Then open it up and dissect it into cause, matter, purpose and the length of time before it must end.*

Marcus Aurelieus, Roman general, philosopher

## Understand the Level of the problem

You can then assess how urgently a solution is needed. Ask questions to establish:

→ Has there been a major accident, is anyone hurt?

→ Is there a legal problem involving a third party such as a supplier?

→ Who is involved – your main clients, stakeholders or influencers, the press?

→ Can the organisation continue until a strategic solution is found or is immediate action necessary?

## Next understand the Operational impact

→ What has brought this to our attention?

→ How much of the organisation is affected?

→ What are the immediate and underlying causes of the difficulty?

→ For how long has this been a problem?

→ What is the likely cost of ignoring this, if that is possible?

→ What steps have we taken before to try either to avoid or solve this problem?

→ What stopped them from working and are those reasons still relevant?

You may need to repeat the question about underlying causes to be certain that you have a complete picture. There may have been good reasons for the original decisions so be careful to check that these are no longer relevant before you decide to change them. Get your facts from people working in the part of the organisation where the problem arose. Remember that managers can sometimes assume that processes and decisions have been made according to the rules, when this might not be the case.

### Now identify the Givens

Find out or review the fixed requirements which cannot be changed:

→ What must we provide and when?

→ At what cost? For example how much resource can we afford day to day on this operation?

→ Who needs to do it? Must that department, region, office or person be involved in handling this process?

→ Are we clear about the assumptions we are making and that these are all valid and essential?

### Trust your Instinct

*Brains first,
then hard work.*

Eeyore in *Winnie-
the-Pooh*, A.A. Milne

If an emerging suggestion feels wrong treat that as a reason to re-examine your assumptions and options. Ask yourself what it is about the suggestion that makes you uneasy – there will be a good reason for your disquiet; you need to identify and act on it.

### Be Creative

The obvious answer may not give you the best result in the long term. Remember that every difficulty provides an opportunity to take the organisation forward – we learn more from mistakes than from successes.

→ What is the ideal solution? How could we make that happen? Does this tell us anything about the 'Givens'?

→ Does this difficulty provide the opportunity to organise the work differently or give someone a development opportunity?

→ Can we use this difficulty to help forge a new partnership or a different relationship?

→ What other options are available?

**Take Action**

As a leader you need to decide and be clear about which option is to be implemented, what you want to happen and when.

→ What is the preferred solution and who else may need to approve it?

→ What is the full cost of implementing it?

→ What is the timescale for implementation?

→ What needs to happen now? Who needs to do what and by when?

→ How can we handle any foreseeable and unforeseen difficulties?

→ Are there any other impacts that we need to consider?

→ How and when do we communicate the changes?

**Learn from experience**

Finally, and very importantly, the leader's role is to ensure that the organisation learns from the experience, otherwise you have not gained any lasting value from the effort involved.

→ Will the proposed solution prevent a repeat of the problem?

→ How long will this solution remain effective?

→ How do we share the learning?

Take care to delegate effectively – allocate the accountability for action and communication clearly and unambiguously to individuals, not teams.

## In practice...

*For disaster recovery and business continuity purposes a property company needed an electronic scan of lease documents that were more than 100 years old. These were in copperplate handwriting on parchment and sealed with sealing wax. They were approximately A1 size portrait and would not go through modern scanning machines.*

*Having analysed the problem using the LOGICAL method, the solution was to use 1970s microfiche technology and photograph the pages. The film could then be stored on a CD and logged on to the computer system, the message being that the most modern and up-to-date methods and techniques do not always work and it is sometimes better to revisit the past.*

## Read around

*The seven habits of highly effective people,* S. Covey

## Links to other leadership tips

**2**   Identify what you want to change or how to spot what is wrong

**80**  Question others

**96**  Distinguish between a business opportunity and a business problem

**99**  Think strategically

# Recharge your BATTERIES

No one can work flat out for long periods without suffering some adverse consequences. Leaders are the individuals who shoulder the load and they can often think that nothing will happen unless they are present at work. This can lead to burn-out.

Treat yourself as you would treat your favourite car. It needs a service now and again, a wash outside and a valeting inside, and it will not go anywhere unless you keep the oil and petrol topped up regularly.

Here are some suggestions to recharge your own batteries:

**1** Find a mentor who is in a leadership position unconnected with your own operation. Identify someone:

→ who has different leadership gifts to you;

→ whom you trust;

→ who is an effective listener and asks questions that make you think;

→ who will give you open and honest feedback;

→ with whom learning would be fun.

**2** Make sure you take enough breaks:

→ maxi-breaks called holidays that last a week or more;

→ midi-breaks that can be as short as half a day or a long weekend;

→ mini-breaks that can last anywhere from a few minutes to a few hours.

Recharge your batteries in a way that reminds you that there may be a bigger picture to consider. Ignore the feelings that make you think that you are indispensable at work or the guilt that makes you feel you should be doing something more useful.

Use these breaks for:

→ relaxation – reading a book, sitting by a lake, meditating, listening to music;

→ recreation – gardening, taking a walk, playing ball or bridge or the piano;

→ exercise – walking, jogging, cycling, swimming, skiing or any team sport;

*The word leisure comes from the Latin root 'licere' that means to permit. Leisure really does mean to permit yourself.*

David B. Posen, psychologist, author

- → hobbies – woodworking, cooking, painting, doing jigsaw puzzles;

- → entertainment – going to a cinema, a theatre, a concert, watching a spectator sport;

- → socialising – visiting or entertaining friends, going to the local pub;

- → personal development – taking a course, learning a skill, reading about a new subject;

- → fun – an impromptu chess session, a game of charades, exploring a new area of town.

Source: adapted from D. Posen, *Always change a losing game*

## In practice...

*Margaret was asked to coach PJ, a high-flying director of a fast-paced and pressured research team as he was perceived by his boss to have 'lost the plot'. It gradually emerged that PJ hadn't had a break or a weekend off for 14 months. Once he recognised this he decided that within the following month he would arrange to take three weeks' holiday and take his wife away. He did so and found that on his return he was able to resolve several difficult issues that had been holding up the team. He commented 'I had forgotten to take care of myself – that is one mistake I will not repeat'.*

## Read around

*Always change a losing game*, D. Posen

## Links to other leadership tips

**42** Undertake your own self-development

**43** Write and implement your own leadership development plan

**54** Get the best from mentoring

# Leadership tip **37**
# Influence your BOSS

*Usually authority can be most effectively softened up gradually.*

Sir Peter White, Admiral

It is your responsibility to sell your own ideas to your boss. It is not her or his responsibility to buy them. If you fail to sell your idea to your boss then either the idea was not good enough to convince or your own sales approach was not adequate for the occasion.

Think through 'the win' for your boss. What are the benefits she or he will derive from the proposed course of action? Approach your boss as you would a customer who is thinking of buying your product.

Training in negotiation skills is a wise investment if you are in the position of having to negotiate with your boss for an extra budget or a change in custom and practice.

There are usually three states of mind in which most people approach their boss with a new idea. They assume that:

1 She or he will not like the idea.

2 An aggressive approach is necessary. One of 'I'd just like to inform you of what I intend to do with my department', look the boss in the eye with an attitude of 'Forbid me if you dare' and then depart.

3 They have the authority, are clear about the 'win' for the business and the boss, and, out of courtesy, they need to ask the boss's permission to adopt a new approach – 'May I do this with my department?'.

The first approach will probably mean that you will do nothing or at best do it half-heartedly. This approach is passive. The second, aggressive approach has the potential to lead to confrontation. The third is assertive and will succeed if the case that precedes the question is good enough to convince.

Source: adapted from Sir Peter White, *Preparing for the top*

## *In practice...*

*Stephen wanted to persuade his boss that he should restructure his team and take on a more strategic role. He feared that his boss would be too busy to be willing to tolerate the disruption this might cause and would see it as extra work.*

*Stephen decided to find out what the boss's top three dilemmas were, how his more strategic input could help with them and how the new structure could help deliver more quickly. By presenting his proposal from that point of view he gained immediate agreement.*

## *Read around*

*Preparing for the top*, Admiral Sir Peter White

## *Links to other leadership tips*

# Leadership tip **38**

# Develop the right side of your BRAIN

*To empty one's mind of all thought and refill the void with a spirit greater than oneself is to extend the mind into a realm not accessible by conventional processes of reason.*

Edward Hill, author of *The language of drawing*

The human brain has two hemispheres which work together to help us solve the constant challenges of day-to-day living. For most people, the left side dominates our thinking because it is there that language and logical thought take place – generally we think in words – and Western education develops left-side thinking.

The right side plays a different role. It looks for patterns, pictures and emotions and is the source of the unexpected 'out of the box' approach and creative new idea. Musicians have long known that it is the right side of the brain that enables them to produce great performances.

Both hemispheres are working in harmony when we are in 'flow' – totally immersed in an activity, achieving excellence and unconscious of the passage of time. Good leadership needs both, so leaders need to develop the ability to access the right side. This takes patience and practice.

Michelangelo described sculpture as chipping away the surplus stone to reveal the shapes within. In the same way, drawing can be understood as the process of marking the boundaries of the space. Most adults do not draw well, so the suggestion that the easiest way to 'switch on' the right side of the brain is to learn to draw is often met with concern, fear of loss of face and resistance. It is nonetheless true.

---

### Draw on the right side of your brain

Try this simple exercise. Copy the picture opposite onto a clean sheet of paper.

Now cover your drawing and take another clean sheet. Turn this book upside down and copy the upside down picture.

Compare the two. Most people find that the second drawing is 'better', either because it is more recognisable or because the proportions are more accurate.

By setting the left side of the brain a puzzle that it couldn't handle logically, you switched it off and allowed the right side to guide your seeing. The right side asked simple questions, 'What is that shape?' and 'Where does the line go?', rather than the left-side approach: 'That is an index finger, so it must look like the index finger image in my mental catalogue'.

143

When faced with a problem at work use right-side thinking:

→ Ask questions such as 'What are we aiming for here?'; 'What does it look like?'; 'What would a good solution sound like?'; 'What would make it more fun?'; 'Why do I feel angry about that?'.

→ Use visualisation techniques and other creative processes; draw a picture of what a great solution would look like. All this will enhance your creativity and help develop new approaches and solutions to old problems.

→ Aim for what seems impossible – 'If it wasn't impossible what would it be like?'. You will be surprised at what you can create.

Source: adapted from B Edwards, *Drawing on the right side of the brain*

## Read around

*Drawing on the right side of the brain*, B. Edwards

## Links to other leadership tips

# Leadership tip 39
## Use business performance COACHING

Performance coaching is now recognised as one of the key approaches to developing engaged and responsible employees and to helping them improve their day-to-day performance at work. Coaching is also a great way of encouraging people to think creatively for themselves, and so is a crucial aspect of effective delegation.

Every conversation at work has the potential to be coaching – a conversation that can result in a shift in the other person's performance. Yet it would not be appropriate for every conversation to be the same. There are times when you need to tell others what has been decided or what is expected of them, other times when your aim is to get them to think a problem through for themselves. Both approaches result in a performance shift, and are coaching conversations.

---

**Assess your coaching skills**

There is a **spectrum of coaching skills** that embraces both extremes:

| DIRECTIVE | solving problems for them | PUSH |
|---|---|---|
| | Telling | |
| | Instructing | |
| | Giving advice | |
| | Offering guidance | |
| | Giving feedback | |
| | Making suggestions | |
| | Asking questions that raise awareness | |
| | Summarising | |
| | Paraphrasing | |
| | Reflecting | |
| | Listening to understand | |
| NON-DIRECTIVE | helping them to solve problems | PULL |

Effective leaders understand the spectrum and use it.

Take a few minutes now to consider the descriptions of the spectrum above. Think about an ordinary day at work and tick the actions you use most frequently. You may find, in common with most people, that your ticks tend towards one half of the list. Knowing that you have the whole spectrum available to you may provide some insight into alternative approaches when dealing with those people or situations where your current approach isn't working.

---

*Each one of us is born with an innate capacity to learn.*

Myles Downey, professional coach, author

*Socrates believed it possible to help people to understand but not to make people understand.*

Max Landsberg, author of *The Tao of coaching*

## When to be directive (push)

When you need to transmit facts and information, do so clearly and unambiguously. There is no point in asking the new recruit where the fire exits might be.

As a leader you will need to explain why change is needed and what it is expected to achieve.

Ask yourself if you are the only one who has all the information. If so tell others. If not, ask.

## When to be non-directive (pull)

When you need to achieve action through others, you will be most effective when you ask them to suggest how best to go about it. Once you have explained the vision you will gain commitment to action and enthusiasm for the task by giving them the chance to take responsibility for it – 'How could we make that work for us?'.

This approach builds confidence, knowledge and self-reliance and so increases capacity in the organisation. It also achieves effective delegation – those whose job it is retain the responsibility for taking action, a key attribute of effective leadership.

## A simple structure for a coaching conversation – the GROW model

A good coaching conversation contains the following elements:

**G**oal – what the coachee wants to achieve from the conversation.

**R**eality – achieving understanding of the current position, who/what/ how much/what have you already tried?

**O**ptions – what the coachee believes might be possible.

**W**rap-up – decision/clarity/commitment/support.

If there is no outcome, it has been a chat, not a coaching conversation.

Key questions to ask are:

→ 'Tell me ... what would you like to get out of this conversation?'

→ 'Ideally, what would you like to happen?'

→ 'Anything else?'

→ 'What might or could you do?'

→ 'What stops you?'

→ 'Anything else?'

→ 'What will you do?. When?' etc.

→ 'On a scale of one to ten, how certain are you that you will do this?'

→ 'What would increase that a little?'

Challenge generalisations: the more you can help the other person to be clear about exactly what is happening now (the current reality) the more options she or he is likely to be able to generate.

If the coachee cannot suggest any options at all try asking what they would like to see happen if anything was possible – wave your magic wand.

As a general rule you will move towards the non-directive end of the spectrum by asking questions rather than making statements. For example, 'We cannot finance that' might become, 'How could we finance that?'.

In a coaching conversation you do not have to accept every suggestion, however keen the other person is on it. You need to use your judgement. Ask yourself if your caution/discomfort is because it is not your preferred solution or the way you would do it, or whether in fact there is a genuine business objection. If the latter, explain the issue and ask how that might be included or addressed.

*Do not ask 'Why?'.* 'Why?' is always followed by 'Because ...'. It immediately creates defensiveness and justification and closes down options. You can always turn 'Why?' into 'What?' – try it!

Effective leaders use the whole spectrum as the occasion demands, and they find more occasions to be non-directive than their ineffective peers.

### Read around

*Coaching for performance*, J. Whitmore

*The inner game of tennis*, T. Gallwey

*The Tao of coaching*, M. Landsberg

### Links to other leadership tips

# Leadership tip **40**

# **Understand and deal with CONFLICT at work**

Dealing with conflict is an essential skill of a good leader and it is one of the aspects of leadership which most people find challenging.

Once you have recognised that someone is 'difficult', or that a particular situation is likely to cause conflict, stop and analyse what it is that makes you think so.

It may be because others:

→ have a different agenda;

→ approach work from a different perspective;

→ are very stressed;

→ don't have the skills needed to do the job;

→ see you as a threat to their personal power or standing;

→ believe that you don't have the skills to do your job.

*We do not see things
as they are, we see
them as we are.*

The Talmud

It will seldom be because people just enjoy being difficult. If you think that this is the root cause, bear in mind that it must have been a successful strategy for them in the past and has meant that they have succeeded in getting their own way. So think about what they have gained and whether you can either live with that or find an alternative which meets the needs of you both.

Whatever the reason you identify for the conflict, ask yourself these questions:

→ What do I want and why do I want and need it?

→ Is this essential to the business and the organisation or is it just my personal preference?

→ What is it about this person/situation that I find difficult? Is it about one task or behaviour or does it occur in certain circumstances?

→ What does the other person need to get out of the meeting?

→ Do the others understand what I need? (Have I explained?)

→ How can we both/all get what we need?

→ How can I present my request in a way that maintains the self-esteem of the other person(s)?

Most conflict arises from misunderstanding and poor communication. If both 'sides' understand each other's agenda you are much more likely to achieve a successful outcome.

## *In practice...*

*Jo, the managing director of a medium-sized hotel, had continuing difficulty with one of her senior managers who was constantly negative, resisted suggestions and seldom met agreed targets. Jane decided to take her away from the hotel for a day. They visited a National Trust property, a shared interest, and then had lunch. After the meal Jo explained how she was feeling about their relationship, the behaviour she found hard to deal with and her disappointment that previous good performance had deteriorated in recent months. She asked the manager for her help in resolving their difficult working relationship.*

*The manager explained that she had been feeling slighted because someone else had been given a job she wanted and she feared for her prospects in the company. She had not realised that she was seen as negative and obstructive. Jo was able to explain and reassure her – in fact the company had plans to expand the manager's work area and, provided performance returned to its previous good level, she would be in line for promotion. They agreed a series of actions and feedback sessions over the next few months to check that progress was back on track.*

*Jo told us that she had been very worried about the discussion beforehand but had found it the most useful meeting she had ever had at work. The manager had given her some helpful feedback too, as she realised that she hadn't explained the big picture to her senior team and some of the others were also worried.*

## *Read around*

*Assertiveness at work*, K. and K. Back

## *Links to other leadership tips*

# Recognise and use the differences between DEBATE and DIALOGUE

There are occasions at work when we need the competitive behaviours of debate and there are other times when we need the more reflective skills of dialogue. One is not bad and the other good. Both are needed for complete leadership.

| Debate | Dialogue |
|---|---|
| Winning and losing | Winning and winning |
| Judgemental | Judgement suspended |
| Only own opinions are important | Valuing differences in opinion |
| Listening<br>– to interrupt<br>– to await your turn to speak<br>– for agreement or disagreement<br>– for the formula or the flaw | Really listening<br>– first to understand,<br>  then seeking to be understood<br>– to learn<br>– to apply to you |
| Hiding your feelings | Speaking your truth |
| Justifying and defending assumptions | Inquiring into assumptions |
| No reflection | Time for reflection |
| Resisting the tide | Going with the flow |
| Seeing distinctions | Seeing connections |
| Asking leading questions | Asking open questions |
| Thinking automatically | Thinking about your thinking |
| One right answer | Paradoxically many right answers |
| Telling, selling, persuading | Learning through inquiry<br>and disclosure |

Source: L. Ellinor and G. Gerrard, *Dialogue*

*Socrates changed an earlier method of discourse, designed for winning an argument, into a method of learning. In the process he created the quintessential model for questioning and learning in the Western world.*

Sally J. Goerne, scientist, author

## *In practice...*

*Andrew was charged with arriving at a satisfactory salary negotiation agreement with the trade unions in a financial services company. He used all the techniques of dialogue in order to establish the position of the officials representing the members.*

*He then referred to the CEO and was told that in no circumstances could the company afford a settlement of more than nine per cent. He commented at the time how amazingly clear the problem had become when faced with only one solution. He then used the techniques of debate in order to arrive at a solution that would match the objectives of his CEO. Within the overall limit they discovered sufficient flexibilities to be able to meet the majority of the trade union demands and reach an agreed settlement. The techniques of debate are as useful as those of dialogue.*

## *Read around*

*Dialogue*, L. Ellinor and G. Gerrard

## *Links to other leadership tips*

**27** Value the differences in people

**40** Understand and deal with conflict at work

**47** Build your self-esteem without becoming arrogant

## Leadership tip **42**

# Undertake your own self-DEVELOPMENT

Taking time out for one's own self-development involves concentrating on what is important but not urgent. If we do not concentrate on what is important, the necessary action will become urgent. If you cannot take the time to be healthy you had better make the time to be ill.

Most philosophies in life deal explicitly or implicitly with four dimensions of self-development. These represent a significant investment in our own lives and in the future contribution we can potentially to make to society.

**1  Physical**

→ Ensure that we have enough physical endurance, body flexibility and strength to live to our full potential.

→ Practise good nutritional habits.

→ Manage our own stress.

**2  Mental**

→ Continue to learn throughout life.

→ Recognise that there is more in the box entitled 'I don't know' than there is in the box entitled 'I know'.

→ And that there is even more in the box 'I don't know what I don't know'.

**3  Social or emotional**

→ Our emotional life is primarily developed out of, or manifested in, our relationships with others.

→ Invest time in relationships for the sake of the relationship rather than for what we want out of the relationship.

**4  Spiritual**

→ Spend time in clarifying personal vision and values so that the bigger picture is always on your personal agenda.

→ Consciously seek a sense of peace and well being.

Source: adapted from S. Covey, *The seven habits of highly effective people*

*If you are not working on yourself, you're not working.*

Ray Noyes, businessman, jazz pianist, Buddhist

153

## *In practice...*

*Peter, a charity CEO, told us that he was getting bored at work as there were no new challenges.*

*When we challenged him on each of the above four dimensions he discovered that he hadn't learned anything new for several years, he had never explicitly identified his values and that he had given up playing squash because he had decided that he was too old.*

*Recognising these gaps enabled him to decide to join the local tennis club, identify his values and as a result volunteer as a mentor to new CEOs.*

*Six months later he told us that he was much too busy to be bored and that his mentee had given him some useful tips that he had used in his organisation!*

## *Read around*

*The seven habits of highly effective people, S. Covey*

## *Links to other leadership tips*

**36** Recharge your batteries

**43** Write and implement your own leadership development plan

**65** Spend your time wisely as a leader

## Leadership tip **43**

# Write and implement your own leadership DEVELOPMENT plan

Follow the steps below to produce an achievable action plan that will enhance your leadership skills.

1  A leadership action plan is about personal commitment. Commitment produces the daily triumph of integrity over scepticism. You can only act for yourself; you cannot act for anyone else.

2  Bear in mind the need for a balance in life. Before you affirm to do anything you should look at yourself as a total person. Success in leadership is not all about work.

3  Action plans are positive – they are not about behaviour you choose to leave behind. 'I promise to give up smoking' is no good. 'I will identify the times when I feel under stress and need a cigarette and record them' is much better.

4  Make action plans SMART – specific, measurable, action orientated, realistic and time bound. If an action needs to be more than one sentence, make two affirmations.

5  Development plans should be written in an achieved manner, 'I will have completed a negotiation skills course by October 1'.

6  Put in action words that trigger movement. Use adverbs that describe how the goal will be achieved. 'By March 20th, I will have successfully organised the sales and marketing seminar.'

7  Chunk the action down until it is realistic. Fluent German cannot be learned from zero knowledge of the language by next Tuesday. 'By next Tuesday I will have identified a German language school to approach for advice.'

8  Do not compare yourself with others. Do not affirm to be like someone else. Choose the skill or the quality to which you aspire and affirm to acquire it. 'By August 17th I will have identified the skills and qualities that make Joanne a successful leader and set my goals to acquire them.'

**10** Courage is the ability genuinely to commit to a target or a course of action without knowing how to achieve it. Courage is acting in spite of the fear of failure. 'By the end of the year I have committed to increasing the sales of my department by 15%. Although as yet I do not know how to achieve this, by the end of next month I will have worked out the steps that need to be taken.'

Source: adapted from L. Tice, *New age thinking for achieving your potential*

| Learning point | Affirmation |
|---|---|
| **1. Knowledge areas** | |
| Increase my knowledge of the Myers Briggs Type Indicator | By October I will have successfully completed the basic programme and applied it to six different coaching situations. |
| **2. Skills** | |
| Basic sign language for deaf people | By the end of 2008 I will have attended and successfully completed the Institute for the Deaf 'Signing for Beginners' course. |
| **3. Behaviours** | |
| Walking the job | By April 14th I will have diarised a system whereby I arrive at work 10 minutes early at the various locations where my staff work and use the time to walk the job and really listen to them. |

## Read around

*New age thinking for achieving your potential*, L. Tice

## Links to other leadership tips

**36** Recharge your batteries

**42** Undertake your own self-development

**65** Spend your time wisely as a leader

# How to have a successful meeting with a DIFFICULT person

People whom you see as difficult are usually behaving in that way for one or more of three reasons:

1  They have an unresolved grievance.

2  They have a different style of thinking, acting and being; for example, a leader whose strongest suit is that of a warrior may have difficulty dealing with a person whose strongest suit is that of a lover, and vice versa.

3  They have developed a coping strategy of being difficult as this has proved successful in the past.

Whatever the reason for the behaviour there are some key steps you need to bear in mind.

→ Where a grievance procedure exists, and most organisations have one, ensure that you have read, learned and thoroughly understood the ramifications of all of the stages. Ensure that you stick to the procedures laid down and carefully record everything that is required.

→ At the outset, be clear about what you and the other person need from the discussion and how this contributes to delivering the organisational vision.

→ Use negotiation techniques and work out the win for the other person as well as for yourself.

→ If you have made a mistake, or you know you have not achieved something, acknowledge this at the outset. 'I know that I didn't give you enough information yesterday, I hope that you now have all that you need.' Never use this as a ploy.

→ If you are criticised, use an assertiveness technique called 'fogging'. Thank your opponent for the criticism and do not question it further or attempt to justify it. 'That is useful to know. Thank you for the feedback.'

→ If the other person starts attacking you verbally or keeps changing the subject, try the 'broken record technique' – keep repeating the reason for the meeting and your own main request.

*No one can make you feel inferior without your consent.*

Eleanor Roosevelt, former First Lady, author

→ Keep your behaviour under control. It is useful to disclose your feelings – 'I am finding this conversation difficult'; 'I feel angry/hurt/upset' – but do it in a calm and collected way.

→ Apportioning blame usually brings about justification and the situation worsens. Take responsibility for what is your fault, avoid personal criticism of the other party and speak objectively about the issue in hand – 'We need to find a solution to the orders backlog'.

→ Ask the other person for their suggestions about handling the difficulty – 'How do you think we might sort this out?'; 'What would you suggest we do about it?'.

→ If you suspect that an unresolved grievance exists that has not been made formal, it is good practice to suggest that the grievance procedure is invoked. Even if your suggestion is declined the invitation to do so should be recorded. It will demonstrate your objectivity and even-handedness and will protect you in case you need to revisit this later.

→ Close the meeting on a civilised note, even if it has not been positive. Be courteous; thank them for their time and use the exit door quietly if you have caught the difficult person on a bad day or at the wrong time.

→ If emotions run too high suggest a break and a time to meet again later.

→ Rehearse, rehearse, rehearse.

## In practice...

*Jane once worked for a man who enjoyed bullying his staff. She had been finding the experience increasingly debilitating and feared that one day she would become inappropriately angry and thereby give him ammunition to use against her.*

*Jane decided to raise the issue at her next appraisal meeting. She was very concerned at how he might react but concluded that if she couldn't resolve the problem she would leave the job.*

*Jane explained that she wanted to talk about how she was feeling about working there, the specific difficulties she was having and the hope she had that they could find a way of getting the best out of the working relationship.*

*Jane was careful to stick to her own knowledge and not to generalise. The manager was sarcastic throughout and constantly interrupted. Jane stuck to what she had rehearsed and at the end asked him what he would do if he was her. He told Jane to put up or get out. By that he meant complain to his boss or leave. She did both. The manager was sacked but it was an unpleasant time for everyone.*

## Read around

*Assertiveness at work*, K. and K. Back

Your own grievance and disciplinary procedures

## Links to other leadership tips

**40** Understand and deal with conflict at work

**41** Recognise and use the difference between debate and dialogue

**55** Negotiate

## Leadership tip **45**
# Survive those moments of self-DOUBT

Leadership is often tough. Responsibilities can be enormous and they may embrace circumstances that could not have been foreseen. Leaders have to make far bigger decisions than anyone else around them – particularly where people are involved. Sometimes the very difficult decisions have to be made alone and can be resolved only after the most profound, painful and inescapable soul searching.

Leaders often have doubts of their own abilities to deal with such situations. In private moments an acute sense of personal inadequacy may overwhelm us.

**Tips for handling those moments of self-doubt**

→ Go back to the vision you created and recall the hope and inspiration you possessed at that time.

→ Examine your own leadership values and apply them to the current situation.

→ Find a wise, respected and trusted person unconnected with your own organisation. Unburden yourself. This will help you acknowledge and examine calmly the dark shadows of inadequacy that exist within us all.

→ Ask yourself 'What is it within me that may be preventing the achievement of the desired objective?'.

→ Imagine how other respected leaders may have tackled similar issues. How would Nelson Mandela have handled this situation, or Anita Roddick or Richard Branson?

→ Go to a place of peace and serenity and reflect upon the truth that every leader in a position of true responsibility has had to face what you are facing.

→ Cast aside the troubles of today and project yourself forward, a week, a month or a year – what will today's troubles look, sound and feel like then?

→ Remind yourself of all the things that are going right and draw strength and resolution from them.

*In times of great adversity it is best to plough your energies into something positive.*

Lee Iacocca, industrialist

## In practice...

*In 1996 Brian resigned from corporate life to begin his freelance career. As part of the resignation process, even as a director of the company, he was summoned to the personnel department, who ran through their checklist asking him to hand over his company car keys, his Amex card, his staff pass, his BUPA membership card and his airmiles card.*

*It suddenly hit him. He thought 'what right have I got to deprive my family of all this security?'. The thought was paralysing for 24 hours.*

*Brian is still freelance 10 years later.*

## Read around

*Feel the fear and do it anyway*, S. Jeffers

*Inspirational leadership*, R. Olivier

## Links to other leadership tips

# Leadership tip **46**
# Develop your EMOTIONAL INTELLIGENCE

Daniel Goleman in his book on this subject defines emotional intelligence as the ability to:

### Recognise your own feelings

Self-awareness is the ability to monitor feelings from moment to moment. It is crucial to psychological insight and self-understanding. People with greater certainty about their feelings are better pilots of their lives, having a surer sense of how they really feel about personal decisions ranging from whom to marry to what job to take.

### Manage your own emotions

Handling feelings so that they are appropriate is an ability that builds on self-awareness. We all need the ability to soothe ourselves, to shake off anxiety, gloom or irritability. People who are poor at this ability are constantly battling against feelings of distress, while those who excel can bounce back more quickly from life's setbacks.

### Motivate yourself

Marshalling emotions in the service of a goal is essential for paying attention, for self-motivation, mastery and creativity. Emotional self-control – delaying gratification and stifling impulsiveness – underlies accomplishment of every sort. People who have this skill tend to be more productive and effective at whatever they undertake.

### Recognise feelings in others

Empathy is a fundamental 'people' skill. People who are empathetic are more attuned to the subtle social signals that indicate what others need or want. This makes them better at vocations such as the caring professions, teaching, sales, coaching and leadership.

### Manage relationships and motivate others

The art of relationships is, in large part, a skill in influencing the emotions of others. These are the abilities that underlie leadership and personal effectiveness. People who excel at these attributes do well at anything that relies on smooth interactions.

Source: D. Goleman, *Emotional intelligence*

### In practice...

*One way to recognise emotional intelligence is to watch the way that people drive on motorways. A driver with low emotional intelligence is not aware of the effect that a signal to pull out to change lane will have on the people behind his own vehicle. Those behind will think, 'Is he signalling because he intends to pull out straight away?' 'Has he seen me in his rear view mirror?' 'Is he aware that I am approaching?' 'Will he allow me to pass before he pulls out?'. The driver with low emotional intelligence is unaware that he is putting those behind in a quandary and forcing them to make a decision to brake or to accelerate.*

*A driver with high emotional intelligence will wait until there is a gap in the traffic before signalling to pull out because she is aware of the effect that the one simple act of indicating will have on other drivers.*

*Good leaders, just like good drivers, need a high level of emotional intelligence. Good leaders are aware of the effect that their words and actions have on other people.*

### Read around

*Emotional intelligence*, D. Goleman

### Links to other leadership tips

**4** Tell the difference between management and leadership

**9** Use the dyadic or relationship-based approach to leadership

Leadership tip **47**

# Build your self-ESTEEM without becoming arrogant

The dictionary defines self-esteem as 'having a good opinion of yourself'. Put another way, it is the ability to value yourself for who you are and for your skills, attributes and contributions to family, work and society at large. This does not mean being unrealistic or failing to recognise scope for development. It does mean learning to give yourself a pat on the back, to say sorry when needed and to laugh at yourself occasionally.

It is important for leaders to develop their self-esteem, as people have difficulty trusting and following those who don't trust or believe in themselves.

**Pay attention to three key areas.**

### 1. Take time to notice what you have achieved

→ Make a habit of taking time after meetings to reflect on what went well. It might be that you persuaded someone of your view or that you spoke to someone you wanted to meet. It doesn't have to be a major breakthrough, just notice what went well.

→ Take time at regular intervals to remind yourself of your values and to congratulate yourself on how you are living these at work.

→ Listen to your intuition as well as to your conscious mind and recognise when this has paid dividends for you and/or the organisation.

→ Let your leadership speak for you, and use formal processes such as performance appraisals to list your achievements.

→ Set an example in the way you treat yourself and others and let people know what you expect. Nobody should accept abuse or ridicule.

*Leaders live for success, yet they should be humble when the accolades start to flow.*

Roger Fulton, author

## 2. Develop a sense of proportion

→ Making a mistake doesn't mean you are a bad person – it just means you made a mistake. Ask yourself if the world will end as a result of it, or the organisation will crash, or the roof will fall in, and so on. Measure it against the real scale of disasters. Who will remember next week or next month?

→ Set yourself clear goals that match your competencies but stretch you at the same time and recognise when you have achieved them.

→ When people say 'No' to you, recognise that they are declining a request, not rejecting you as a person.

→ Treat your body well – it is the only one you have and needs the best fuel and regular servicing, just like your car. Taking holidays is not skiving.

## 3. See the lighter side

→ Spend time with people you esteem – let them set you an example. Enjoy their fun and laughter – they are good medicine.

→ Find a place of beauty that gives you peace and serenity.

→ See the funny side of life and work – for example there are lots of hilarious signs around once you begin to notice them. A favourite is 'This building is alarmed' – who frightened it?… And consultant-speak provides rich pickings: 'Meet with yourself regularly' – perhaps we could try meeting without ourselves, could we get twice as much done?!

→ Don't take yourself too seriously. When you look back on your life you will value family, friends and laughter. You will not wish you had spent more time at the office.

## *In practice...*

*Brian was once given a bookmark for Christmas. The legend on it was, 'Piss off; I know I'm right'. He realised that this was a message that perhaps he needed to be perceived as rather less arrogant and less 'right' in many situations. At this turning point he committed to using the techniques of 'dialogue' instead of his more usual approach of 'debate'.*

## Read around

*Common sense leadership*, R. Fulton

*Feel the fear and do it anyway*, S. Jeffers

*Overcoming low self-esteem*, M. Fennell

## Links to other leadership tips

# Get into that state of ultra-high performance known as FLOW

It is the job of a leader to extract the best possible performance from individuals and teams. Best possible performance happens for an individual when there is no conscious effort put into a task and yet the results are superb. This can happen while giving a presentation, writing a report or designing a computer program. The individual is so absorbed that time becomes irrelevant.

This state can happen to teams of individuals who are so in tune both with the task they are performing and with each other that they effortlessly adjust their contributions for the good of the team as a whole without individual preferences getting in the way.

In sport this feeling is known as being 'in the zone'. In the theatre it is called 'peak performance' and a jazz band calls it 'being in sync'. In psychology it is known as the state of flow. Flow is a state of concentration so focused that it amounts to complete absorption in an activity.

Flow has the following characteristics:

→ feeling of strength;

→ alertness;

→ effortless control;

→ unselfconsciousness;

→ at one's peak;

→ transformation of time;

→ it is intrinsic; it cannot be measured externally.

*At bottom, becoming a leader is simply becoming ourselves; it is precisely that simple and precisely that difficult.*

Warren Bennis, professor, author

It is a time of relaxed concentration so the body is not tired by it. In flow we do not sit tensely or rush around being stressed.

To get into flow requires:

→ A challenging activity which needs full attention – routine tasks will not absorb you.

→ Clear goals and feedback – be clear about what you are going to achieve and how you will know when you have done it, e.g., 'I will write the presentation this morning and send it off by lunchtime'.

→ Recognition that this is either important or interesting right now.

→ A reasonably distraction-free environment. Constant callers or telephone calls will break your concentration.

→ Focusing on the task – if you are having trouble focusing ask yourself what you notice about it, what makes it interesting/important just now and what you will achieve as a result of doing it.

→ Relaxing – breathe deeply, don't rush.

Source: M. Csikszentmihalyi, *Flow: the psychology of happiness*

## In practice...

*Brian, Margaret and Ben were engaged to create a written handbook to support a major leadership programme. The way we did this was not planned in advance, it just happened. We even forget who wrote the first piece – but that first piece was so good it set the example for the rest of the material.*

*As authors we worked remotely, we did not even have a meeting. With the benefit of hindsight, we can see that each of us had the same clear vision of what the output should look like and we adapted our individual writing styles to meet the standard required. Within a month the three of us, working independently at our own computers, completed and presented 80 pages of seamless copy to the client, who was delighted with the result and amazed that it could have been produced in such a short period.*

*This is an example of flow in action and an illustration that a team does not necessarily have to meet face to face for this to happen.*

## Read around

*Flow: the psychology of happiness*, M. Csikszentmihalyi

*Learning to lead*, W. Bennis and J. Goldsmith

## Links to other leadership tips

**16** Think creatively

**17** Think creatively in teams

**85** Get the best out of teams

**93** Engage the whole audience

**95** Generate fun at work

Leadership tip **49**

# Become an INSPIRATIONAL leader

Leaders have to offer followers the hope that the future can be better than the past. To do this, a leader may need to break new ground.

An inspirational leader is one who is himself, or herself, inspired. In order to be inspiring to others a leader needs a vision. A vision is a call to the imagination of others to make a difference. A vision paints a picture of the future. It implies a calling to a cause that is higher than oneself – a service for a community, a product that will be of benefit to humankind, the protection of ecological resources. A leader cannot be inspirational while serving her, or his, own ends.

**Tips for becoming an inspirational leader**

→ Have the moral courage to take a stand and declare that 'We can make a difference'.

→ Construct a vision that is short, succinct, memorable and inspiring. It should create an image that provides hope for others.

→ Act as though the vision is already a reality.

→ Believe that you have the necessary leadership qualities. You can't learn about leadership by staying out of it.

→ Aim to share the ownership of the vision with as many people as possible, recognising that there will always be those whom you cannot convince.

→ Recognise that making a difference is inseparable from organisational politics. You will have to 'fight for your corner'.

→ Identify your leadership behaviours in the areas where you are weak and develop them. Do not presume that your strong suits will always carry you through.

→ Be firm and consistent with the cynics, your critics and those who work against you – the traitors.

→ Identify and think carefully about the doubts that lie within yourself.

Source: adapted from a lecture by Richard Olivier

*Whatever you can do, or dream you can, begin it. Boldness has genius, power and magic in it.*

Goethe, poet, philosopher

## *In practice...*

*On 11 September 2001 Margaret was briefing a group of professional peers in preparation for beginning to lead a major leadership programme at one of the Oxford colleges. We were interrupted with the news of the unfolding events in New York and adjourned to watch the live TV reports. Afterwards Margaret had to decide whether to continue, not knowing if this was the beginning of a world conflict. There was no obvious right answer.*

*Margaret stood in front of the group, and had only her values and very basic beliefs to guide her. She shared her sense of horror and her belief that, whatever the outcome, the world was going to need good leadership even more in the future as a result of what had happened. She thought they should continue and deal with the trauma as they went along. For a moment there was complete silence and then everyone started to cheer.*

*It was an astonishing moment and one of the most powerful leadership weeks in Margaret's working life. People told her that she was truly inspirational and even now, years later, still refer to it.*

## *Read around*

*Inspirational leadership*, R. Olivier

## *Links to other leadership tips*

**12** Create a vision for your own operation

**18** Decide your own set of values

**45** Survive those moments of self-doubt

**61** Be a servant leader

Leadership tip **50**

# LEAD for the first time

The biggest challenge in leading for the first time is shifting your own approach from doing it yourself to getting things done through others. You will be tempted to take over various tasks because you can do them quicker, you haven't time to explain, others aren't getting on fast enough or to an acceptable quality standard, or even because you persuade yourself that you are just lending a hand. You must resist this impulse. Remember that all the time you are handling tasks yourself you are:

→ denying others the chance to learn;

→ encouraging upward delegation;

→ increasing unit costs by spending your (expensive) time;

→ not attending to your leadership job.

Whether you are a new CEO or it is your first team leader position, there are three key sets of relationships to which you, as a leader, must pay attention. These are with your boss, your team and yourself.

### Your boss

Spend time finding out what your boss's priorities are and the pressures she or he is under. Understand how your job fits with the rest of the organisation and what the main interactions are. Go and meet the other team leaders and find out from them how your team can help.

If you are the new CEO spend time with the chair, shareholders and key stakeholders. Understand their expectations and priorities.

### Your team

Introduce yourself to the team and make time to meet each individual or group, depending on the numbers involved. Get to know them as people, not just as job descriptions. Explain the organisation's vision and make it relevant to them and their jobs. Remind them of what is expected, and why success matters. Be honest about your expectations around progress, personal appraisals and the feedback you need.

Think about what your team spends time on and how this matches the priorities. This can take time as often the underpinning information is difficult to find. Don't rush into making immediate changes until you are certain that you have consulted all those likely to be affected and those who hold the corporate knowledge – there may be good reasons for some activities, others may be ripe for review.

**Yourself**

→ Be clear about what you want from this job and about the work-leisure balance you need.

→ Draw up a personal leadership development plan and discuss it with your boss.

→ Make time to read about leadership and to attend leadership development events.

→ Find yourself a mentor, someone with whom you can honestly discuss work issues in a completely confidential environment.

→ Decide how long you want to spend in the job and what you will have achieved by then – and review this regularly.

→ When you have achieved what you set out to do and developed your leadership ability, move on.

## In practice...

*Andy, a new CEO, had been brought into an organisation to modernise the systems and refocus it on its long-term goal. After six months there were still systems difficulties and the new accounting system had developed teething troubles. He told me that he was beginning to wonder if he had bitten off more than he could chew or even made things worse.*

*I asked him to remind me why he had taken the job and whether he would do so now knowing what he knew. After some thought he began to tell me about all the things that they had achieved and to remind himself of how far they had come. He told me, with a smile, that the budget would be more than balanced within the year and that he had approval to recruit a new deputy to take some of the load from him.*

*'Actually, it's amazing what we have achieved in such a short time', he said.*

### Read around

*Skills for new managers*, M. Stettner

### Links to other leadership tips

# Leadership tip **51**

# LEAD when you are not an appointed leader

*You become free by acting free.*

Lech Walesa, shipyard worker, Solidarity leader

Making yourself a leader when you aren't one does not mean running around shouting 'I'm in charge'. You become a leader by acting like a leader. You only need to be willing to embrace responsibility, to be able to elicit the cooperation of others, listen to their needs and then place those needs above your needs.

Change can take place because people who are not in positions of authority take on the leadership role and lead other like-minded people towards a desirable goal.

### In practice...

*Lech Walesa was not in a position of authority in Poland. He was a humble shipyard worker. Nevertheless he founded the Solidarity movement and led Poland from the restraining shackles of communism.*

Even the simplest of things needs changing or improving. What in your work environment needs changing for the better?

→ Does the workplace need cleaning up or making more cheerful?

→ Does the stationery cupboard need reorganising?

→ Does the Christmas party need a new approach?

→ Does the team logo need revitalising?

→ Can you involve your team in a community project?

→ Does the organisation's newsletter need improving? If there isn't one why not start one?

If you decide to take on the leadership mantle for any change...

→ ...**always** ask for permission on behalf of the group, never for yourself;

→ ...**never** pick a fight with your boss.

## Read around

*How to win friends and influence people,* D. Carnegie

## Links to other leadership tips

## Leadership tip **52**
# Lead a fulfilling LIFE as a leader

*To know how to live is all my calling and my art.*

Molière, French author

There are said to be seven main ingredients in the recipe for a fulfilling life:

1  **Good health** – this involves a level of vitality that goes far beyond freedom from illness. It means boundless energy and enthusiasm for life.

2  **Material sufficiency** – which means having enough resources for your needs and not having to spend time and energy worrying about money.

3  **Loving relationships** – for which you need the ability to get along with others, to listen and express yourself well, accept people as they are and make them feel special and an appreciation of how you can best contribute to the growth of others.

4  **Being able to live as you wish** – to be in control of the direction of your life, pursuing your interests and talents and making your own choices.

5  **A sense of purpose and fulfilment** – a deep inner knowledge that your life has some meaning. A conviction that you know where you are going and how you are going to get there.

6  **Peace of mind** – the ability to feel good about yourself all the time, a genuine liking for yourself.

7  **A belief that you will leave the world a better place than you found it** – you will be leaving a legacy and have the satisfaction of knowing that you have made a valuable contribution.

Source: adapted from R. Johnson and D. Swindley, *Awaken your inner power*

### *In practice...*

*After a very successful career in the world of commerce, Bill achieved his lifetime ambition after he retired and he was in his 70s. He was elected to the synod of the Church of England – which for him was the ultimate accolade.*

### Read around

*Awaken your inner power,* R. Johnson and D. Swindley

*To have or to be,* E. Fromm

### Links to other leadership tips

**9**   Use the dyadic or relationship-based approach to leadership

**12**   Create a vision for your own operation

**18**   Decide your own set of values

**46**   Develop your emotional intelligence

**95**   Generate fun at work

# Leadership tip **53**
# **Really LISTEN**

*Star leaders listen with rapt attention. They have a way of making you feel that you are the most important human being in the universe for the five or thirty five minutes you spend with them.*

Tom Peters, business guru, author

Somebody taught all of us to talk, somebody taught all of us to read, somebody taught us to write, but only professional counsellors are taught how to listen.

Most of us listen:

→ for what we already know;

→ for what we agree with;

→ for what we disagree with;

→ to await for our turn to speak;

→ to interrupt;

→ to look or sound good;

→ for the answer;

→ for the formula;

→ for the flaw in the argument.

We do not listen authentically.

## Purpose

The purpose of listening is to understand the thoughts, opinions, ideas and feelings of others by focusing on their agenda rather than one's own.

Listening is an active skill. It requires practice and concentration. There are eight main ways to demonstrate the generosity of your listening.

**1** Establish eye contact and display an active body language to show people that they have your full attention.

**2** Concentrate on the content of what they are saying rather than the delivery.

**3** Listen *between* the words as well as *to* the words.

**4** Resist your own need to comment.

**5** Reflect back what they have actually said without evaluation.

**6** Reflect back their feelings – 'I can see you are angry and upset'.

**7** Summarise and rephrase what has been said to ensure that you have understood.

**8** Interpret what has been agreed.

### In practice...

*Alan, a civil servant, had been finding that meetings with his senior team appeared to make good decisions but additional information kept turning up afterwards, which caused problems. He decided to change his approach and not give his opinion at the outset. He confined himself to asking questions to get as much information as possible from those present. He was very surprised at how difficult it was to rein himself in and even more surprised at how effective the approach turned out to be. 'I had no idea how good the team really are. I'm finding out about things I have been worried about for months and there are very few real problems', he told me.*

### Read around

*The inner game of tennis*, T. Gallwey

### Links to other leadership tips

**39** Use business performance coaching

**72** Consult those affected before making a decision

**76** Give and receive feedback

**80** Question others

# Leadership tip **54**

# **Get the best from MENTORING**

*Mentoring has its origins in the concept of apprenticeship, when an older, more experienced individual passes down his knowledge of how the task should be done and how to operate in the commercial world.*

David Clutterbuck, author

### What is mentoring?

There is no generally accepted workplace definition of mentoring. Like coaching, it has the attributes of giving time, space and freedom of choice to enable an individual to grow and develop. A mentor generally offers more advice than a coach, giving guidance based on personal knowledge and experience. The mentor is usually a more senior and experienced person who is willing to share his or her own experiences of successes and failures at work, and a knowledge of how organisations function, with a less experienced colleague.

Effective mentoring requires trust and confidentiality between the parties involved and can never take place within a line or matrix management relationship.

The advantages are not all one way. Mentors have the opportunity to develop their listening and coaching skills, gain a fresh insight into their organisation (or to learn about another organisation) and talent spot!

### How do I find a mentor?

Nowadays many large organisations have formal mentoring schemes as part of their leadership and management development arrangements. A mentor from the same organisation can be a valuable source of information about senior team thinking (and politics) and can bring the mentee to the attention of senior colleagues where appropriate. If an internal mentor is used, it is important to ensure that there is no direct line-management relationship between mentor and mentee or between mentor and mentee's manager.

Many organisations have now set up external mentoring programmes, in which senior people from unconnected organisations take the mentoring role. Mentees in this arrangement gain the advantage of an independent view of their attributes and capabilities and have the opportunity to visit and learn from another organisation.

When choosing a mentor decide if there is particular knowledge or information which would be useful to you, perhaps concerning part of the organisation you haven't worked in.

You will usually be offered one or two names at first with a message from the individuals. You should then arrange to meet informally, away from the desk. If you do not 'take to' the individual, ask for another suggestion. Otherwise agree when, where and how often you will meet.

If your organisation doesn't have a mentoring scheme, ask your professional association/trade union – most can put you in touch with individuals or schemes which can help.

### In practice...

*Tom found that talking to Richard, who was blind, was both challenging and rewarding. Richard would not let Tom get away with the usual generalisations and easy answers. Their relationship developed into mentor/mentee for two real reasons.*

*Firstly, Richard, being blind, was not distracted by Tom's smiles and gestures. He just listened and really heard what Tom said, then asked simple, testing questions. And secondly, he had a completely different perspective on work and life in general from Tom. Tom found this refreshing.*

### Read around

*Mentoring executives and directors*, D. Clutterbuck

### Links to other leadership tips

**39** Use business performance coaching

**67** Develop and maintain trust

# Leadership tip **55**
## NEGOTIATE

All leaders have to learn to negotiate. Because they are interested in changing things for the better they constantly have to negotiate for budget, for the release of staff, for space to experiment or for time.

Negotiation can only take place if there is an overlap of interests and position, as the diagram below shows.

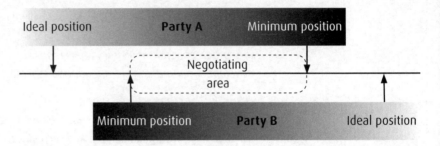

**Ideal position** = the perfect possible case and includes all possible objectives
**Minimum position** = the worst case

**1  Prepare**

→ Create your own list of the issues.

→ Follow each issue with an intention.

→ Find your minimum acceptable position on each issue.

→ Identify the other party's list of issues, intentions and minimum acceptable positions.

**2  Have a dialogue rather than a competitive debate**

→ Review the issues, intentions and positions.

→ Ask direct, open questions; shut up and listen to the answer.

→ Summarise regularly.

**3  Propose**

→ Only proposals can be negotiated. Arguments or opinions cannot.

→ Give them what they want on your terms.

*Give them what they want on your terms.*
Fisher and Ury, authors

→ Ask 'What would make my proposal acceptable?'.

→ Ask 'If my proposal is not acceptable, what is your proposal?'.

**4  Bargain**

→ Put conditions before offers. 'If you do X then I can do Y.'

→ Concede in less important areas to gain in areas of greater importance.

→ Don't throw away 'Elk steaks' in the hope of deterring wolves.

**5  Close and make sure you have agreed what has been agreed**

→ Any ambiguity is cleared up more easily at the time than it is afterwards.

→ Both parties should be happy with the deal.

Source: adapted from R. Fisher and W. Ury, *Getting to yes*

## *In practice...*

*Anne is a professional trainer. On many occasions she has run successful workshops on negotiating skills. At the end of one of them in 1999 she realised that she had not been applying the skills she taught to her own situation. She had merely been accepting the fees offered by the workshop organisers. From then on she negotiated her fees and increased her annual turnover.*

## *Read around*

*Getting to yes,* R. Fisher and W. Ury

## *Links to other leadership tips*

**37** Influence your boss

**40** Understand and deal with conflict at work

**41** Recognise and use the differences between debate and dialogue

**101** Deal with the witchcraft that emanates from head office

# NETWORK as a leader

Networking simply means staying in touch with a wide variety of people in different occupations and sectors, all of whom have a similar outlook to your own. All leaders are good networkers. Some have networks as large as 1,000. To start with, aim to build yours into three figures, all from outside your organisation.

The benefits of spending time networking can occur in the present – someone can give you that one idea you need over lunch. Mostly though, the benefits of networking occur in the future: you are investing now for what you will get back later.

*People who do best have good networks before they need them.*

William Bridges, author of *Creating you & co*

## Purpose

Networking is important to:

→ learn from other leaders;

→ use other leaders to introduce you to yet more leaders;

→ improve your career prospects;

→ make friends who may be able to give you help.

### Steps to maintain existing networks

→ Create a simple database (on the computer or on index cards) of all the people you know in leadership positions. As a minimum this should contain name, address, phone number and e-mail address.

→ Make sure you keep in regular contact with these people by meetings, calls, letters and e-mails. If appropriate, send Christmas and birthday cards.

→ Invest time in the network of relationships for the sake of the relationship, not for what you want out of them.

### Steps to create new contacts

→ Go to as many likely gatherings as possible; recognise that the room is full of people with similar interests, friends you haven't yet met. Talk to as many people as possible and collect business cards. Ask people if you can come and see them. Follow up contacts afterwards.

→ Ask your current network contacts for three introductions – 'If you were me which three people would I need to talk to?'; 'Can I use your name to introduce myself?'. Introductions via e-mail are relatively painless for all parties.

→ Speak on as many public platforms as you can. Make what you have to say relevant, interesting and amusing to the audience.

→ Make people feel special when you meet them. Talk about *their* job not about yours. Listen, listen and listen some more. Be happy and enthusiastic.

→ Engage with the intention of learning at least one new fact, anecdote, opinion or idea in any conversation.

→ Memorise interesting and humorous anecdotes to use in conversation. Make yourself interesting to be with.

→ Send a 'thank you' in the form of handwritten notes rather than formal letters or greetings. This shows that you have taken some time to think about what you are saying.

## *In practice. . .*

*David, newly self-employed, was pleasantly surprised that work seemed just to turn up without advertising. When he thought about how he spent his time he realised that he went to lots of events, professional societies, conferences, and so on and was willing to talk to people about what he did. Networking in that way seemed more like socialising yet it made him visible and known to the community in which he hoped to get business – which was what was needed.*

## *Read around*

*Creating you & co*, W. Bridges

## *Links to other leadership tips*

9    Use the dyadic or relationship-based approach to leadership

# Lead when you are served from a POISONED CHALICE

An organisation that is failing, dying or just waiting for closure needs leadership just as much, if not more so, than a successful operation. If you are offered, or find yourself in, such a no-win situation you have two options.

→ Refuse the leadership role and let the troops fail without you.

→ Embrace the responsibilities of what may seem a hopeless task with a view to maintaining the self-esteem of those who have no choice.

If you do decide the take the role, there are a number of things you should do.

**1** Before you choose to accept, make certain that you have agreed what your role will be and what outcomes you will be accountable for – avoid taking the blame for failing to achieve the perfect transformation. Mark your boss's card with this message.

**2** Meet the people as soon as you have taken over. Make sure they know that things are grim, but that if they give you their support the minimum benefit will be an orderly shutdown and that things could even get better. Give them just a glimmer of hope that tomorrow could be better than today and a timescale for the remaining phase of the operation.

**3** Call in someone from outside to audit the books. This way you know how much money is in the till and then you can decide how it is to be spent.

**4** Pick a short-term goal – a quick win – that you and the team are almost certain to achieve. If this involves spending money you have control over, then spend it; if it involves saving costs, then save costs. Make sure you celebrate the achievement of this goal with the team.

**5** Choose a longer-term goal involving regaining the trust of one key group of stakeholders. These can be customers, head office, shareholders, suppliers, constituents, members etc.

*Do not weep, do not wax indignant. Understand.*

Baruch Spinoza, Dutch philosopher

**6**  Keep a ready antenna on the signals from inside and outside the organisation. Recognise when things are beyond your influence and control. When they are, stick to what you know to be right, the post-mortem will then say you acted prudently and diligently and no one could have done more than you did.

### In practice...

*In the 1980s Margaret was responsible for 'downsizing' an office by just over 50% as a result of a central policy decision. She had argued against it but had failed to persuade the powers that be to make an exception. Some staff would be relocated but many would not. She decided to be completely honest with everyone. At a meeting she told the entire staff what was happening and then met each person individually to discuss the future. In most cases she was able to meet their requests. Some were still unhappy with her decisions, but in the end those who remained understood their value to the organisation and were motivated to make a success of the change.*

### Read around

*Feel the fear and do it anyway*, S. Jeffers

### Links to other leadership tips

**60**  Break the rules and stay in line

## Leadership tip **58**
# Reframe a PROBLEM

One of the main difficulties that we encounter when trying to shift a mindset or to view a problem in a different way is the 'letting go' of the way in which we currently see the problem. The process of 'reframing' gives us a number of different statements about the problem or issue that may help us to re-focus and change the way we approach the process of change.

1   Write down the problem or mindset that you are addressing in simple, straightforward language.

2   Now, write down one alternative statement about the same problem, 'reframing' it in a different way.

3   Come up with several other alternatives.

4   Next, run through an analysis of each of the statements that you have in front of you and think about which approach gives you the best route forwards.

Here are some examples:

a) I am not a creative person; I cannot draw or paint.
b) I need to develop my creative skills so that I can enjoy drawing and painting.

a) My manager never gives me recognition for the work I do.
b) I need to ensure that my manager gives me recognition at work and to tell my manager that it is important for me.

a) I have too much work to do and my work is very stressful.
b) I need to find ways to organise my time better so that when I go home I leave my work in the office.

There are no short cuts. By reframing some of our mindsets, we can start to change our attitudes. This in turn will affect our behaviours. We have the right to choose our attitudes, but we need to know what they are before we can change them. Other people can help us change but we have to take the first steps and believe that the change is worthwhile.

*A habit cannot be tossed out of the window; it must coaxed down the stairs a step at a time.*

Mark Twain, author

## In practice...

*Bob, a quality assurance professional, was very frustrated that he had been unsuccessful in persuading his CEO to introduce additional monitoring and information processes which he believed would make his job easier.*

*When we asked him 'What is in it for the CEO?' he began think about that. He realised that some of his suggestions would not add value to the company overall but also that the core part of his proposal could actually help solve a number of broader problems. He reframed his proposal in that light and achieved his slightly altered, but acceptable, goal.*

## Read around

*Six thinking hats*, E. de Bono

## Links to other leadership tips

**16** Think creatively

**17** Think creatively in teams

**35** Analyse problems

**95** Generate fun at work

**99** Think strategically

# How best to RESIGN

*Never burn a bridge.*

Jim Graves, consultant

When it comes to leaving your job, however tempting you may find the two-fingered salute, or the verbal equivalent, you should not let your emotions get the better of you. You may have landed the job of your dreams, but you never know when your career may bring you back into contact with your former employers. For instance, at some future point they could become a potential client.

**Do:**

→ Tell your immediate boss informally and face to face before handing in a formal letter.

→ Give constructive criticism if necessary but avoid all insults.

→ Be prepared to consider a counter offer from your employers.

→ Do as much as you can to ensure a smooth handover.

→ Remember that the people you are working with could be good future contacts.

→ Choose your referee from amongst your current employers with care (you will almost always need one) and brief them on why you think that you are suitable for the new job.

**Do not:**

→ Resign when you are angry. Do it when you can be both professional and strong.

→ Focus solely on negative points.

→ Feel obliged to give specific reasons for your resignation.

If your employer comes up with a counter offer to make you stay:

→ Consider why it took a threat of resignation to bring it about.

→ Your boss may promise to rectify the problems that may have influenced your resignation decision but how sure can you be that these will be effectively dealt with?

→ If you do decide to stay, your boss may consider you as 'the one who nearly left' and you may find yourself having to re-prove your commitment to the organisation.

→ By staying you will have to turn down a job that you have accepted and this could turn against you if you have to deal with your would-be employer in the future.

## What should I say in my letter of resignation?

→ This letter is a vital part of the resignation process, but it should not be used to air your grievances.

→ It need only state the position from which you are resigning and your intended leaving date.

→ If you wish to add more, keep it positive and resist the temptation to get personal. If you are at all in doubt get someone you trust to read it and advise you.

## What about my notice period?

→ Your notice period will usually be stated in your contract of employment. Where no notice period is stated, work on the basis of one month to allow a responsible handover of your responsibilities.

→ If you wish to exit more swiftly, offer solutions to obstacles that could prevent you. For example draw up a schedule for the completion of all outstanding projects.

→ You may need to include a waiver in your letter of resignation:

'I am aware that my contract demands a notice period of (x) month(s), but I am required by my new employer to start as soon as possible. If you are prepared to waive my notice period, I will be prepared to find ways of helping to hand over to my replacement as soon as he or she is in position.'

## Should I leave before I have another job?

→ Consider the financial implications carefully.

→ Also consider that most employers like to recruit from amongst those still in employment.

→ However, many people do leave work to take a long vacation, to travel, to go to university or just to take time out to reflect what went wrong with their current job.

## Read around

*Kick start your career,* J. Grout and S. Perrin

## Links to other leadership tips

Leadership tip **60**

# Break the RULES and stay in line

Rules are a necessary part of belonging to an organisation and a necessary part of the fabric of being part of society. Rules can be formal or informal. Most formal rules are drafted for a serious purpose. They are there to prevent individuals committing illegal or fraudulent acts. For example a disciplinary procedure has rules that are designed to keep organisational managers out of industrial tribunals. Or rules exist to see that everyone is kept informed, for example to prevent staff offending money laundering obligations.

It is usually imprudent to break a formal rule without careful consideration and without permission from the guardians of the rules. If it is absolutely necessary and you have no time to request permission, then you must have a cast iron reason to do so.

You must also ensure that the actions you are taking in breaking the rules do result in a successful outcome. Breaking the rules and failing almost always is a fast track to the P45.

### *In practice...*

*In the film* Twelve o'clock high*, which was based on real Second World War experiences, the lonely decisions that have to be taken by leaders in war-time situations are portrayed.*

*In one scene, the commander of a failing bomber squadron ignores the order for his group to return to base because visibility was improving and there was the danger of enemy fighter activity. He proceeds with the mission and successfully bombs the intended target without losing any of his aircraft.*

*Upon his return he is carpeted by his commanding officer and, with tongue in cheek, reports that he experienced radio malfunction and did not hear the order to return. It then becomes apparent that he took the decision to break the rules in order to prove to his bomb group personnel that they could accurately and successfully bomb a target when no other group could get through. This was a defining moment, at which the morale of this previously failing organisation was built. The officer had a cast-iron excuse for breaking the rules and was congratulated for so doing.*

*The officer got away with it because the raid was successful. Had he failed, a full military investigation would have ensued.*

In contrast, almost all organisations have informal rules that amount to 'This is the way we do things around here'. These rules did once have a purpose and may still have one today, but many do not. These are the sorts of rules that can be subjected to creative thinking.

Ask yourself:

→ If we were starting from scratch how would we arrange things around here?

→ If we could wave a magic wand, how could things around here look?

→ Imagine emptying your house and putting all your possessions, however big or small, into the garden. Then you can question the need for every item before it is brought back in through the front door. How can we use this analogy and apply it to the way we do things at work?

This is the way that informal rules can be challenged. However, common courtesy dictates that everyone affected by the changes you intend to bring about should be consulted if possible and, as a minimum, kept informed. We should not be in the business of giving work colleagues unpleasant shocks. This is not the way to build trust.

It is vitally important to stay in line when you want to break rules.

Two of the most common informal rules are:

→ Thou shalt not overspend on budget because this will have ramifications for others in the organisation.

→ Thou shalt not underspend on budget because that will give the planners the chance to reduce the budget next time around.

In both cases, if you are in danger of breaking the rules, early notice, together with reasons and what you are proposing to do as a result, should given to all concerned.

### Read around

*Twelve o'clock high*, film available on video and DVD

Any written statement of your own organisational standards, policies or rules

### Links to other leadership tips

## Leadership tip **61**

# Be a SERVANT leader

*Serve to lead.*

Leadership credo
at Sandhurst

Servant leadership is the opposite of traditional command and control management. Servant leaders see themselves as in the service of the greater good of the organisation and see the leader's job as enabling other people to succeed. It is founded on a sense of the interconnectedness of life and all its enterprises.

Servant leaders are driven by their deeply held values, among which is a belief in the potential of others. Although we are free agents, we also have a responsibility for our planet, the environment, our fellow human beings and to provide a future for our children.

This does not mean that servant leaders are 'soft' or 'woolly'. Often quite the contrary – they have very clear standards and expect everyone, including themselves, to live up to them, and can, on occasion, be ruthless with those who do not.

To be a servant leader requires:

→ Being conscious of important, deeply held personal values which include those such as compassion, humility and gratitude – 'I am willing to stand for my beliefs'.

→ Belief in the vision of the organisation – 'I know what I ultimately serve and that business is a part of the larger and much richer fabric of the whole universe'.

→ Determination to achieve the organisational outcomes to build a better future – 'I know that we are ultimately contributing to the quality of life for our people, their families and the wider community'.

→ Subjugation of personal ambition to the greater good of the organisation – 'I have a sense of personal responsibility for the organisation and for taking action. If change is needed I must begin it and model it. If this product or service is to be provided, I have to provide it or I have to persuade others to provide it because it is a good idea'.

→ Viewing the role of leadership as enabling others – 'I cooperate and communicate to build effective relationships throughout and beyond the organisation'.

→ Belief in the potential of people to succeed – I help to make reality happen but cannot always predict the outcome of every initiative'.

Servant leadership is about being aware of the bigger picture as well as doing the job.

## In practice...

'Wells Fargo began its fifteen-year stint of spectacular performance in 1983, but the foundation of the shift dated back to the early 1970s, when the then-CEO, Dick Cooley, began building one of the most talented management teams in the industry.

Cooley foresaw that the banking industry would eventually undergo wrenching change, but he did not pretend to know what form that change would take. So instead of mapping out a strategy for change, he and Chairman Ernie Arbuckle focused on "injecting an endless stream of talent" directly into the veins of the company. They hired outstanding people whenever and wherever they found them, often without any specific job in mind. "That's how you build the future" he said. "If I'm not smart enough to see the changes that are coming, they will. And they'll be flexible enough to deal with them."

At a time when its sector of the banking industry fell 59% behind the general stock market, Wells Fargo outperformed the market by over three times.'

Source: J. Collins, *Good to great*

## Read around

*Good to great*, J. Collins

## Links to other leadership tips

**12** Create a vision for your own operation

**18** Decide your own set of values

**25** Embed new behaviours in line with the values in your organisation

**49** Become an inspirational leader

# Leadership tip 62

## Manage your own STRESS

*Practise 'Shruggism' – shrug both shoulders and think if it happens – so what!*

Dr John Edmondson, consultant behavioural psychotherapist

Stress and leadership go hand in hand because leaders are trying to change things for the better and change means that people will dislike some of the proposed actions. There will be days when you will not be able to get people to do the things you want them to do. There will be others when an unpredicted event ruins all of your plans.

**A stress toolkit**

→ Make an inventory of the things that are causing you stress. Cross out the things that you really cannot change.

→ Tackle one issue at a time.

→ If appropriate, find someone to talk to about the issue causing you stress.

→ Take responsibility for your own stress. Only you can do something about it. Others can help but they can't solve your problem.

→ Set yourself achievable goals rather than impossible ones.

→ Project yourself forward. How do you think you will feel about this situation in one week, one month, or one year's time?

→ Break things down into bite-sized chunks and then do the easiest tasks first. Take that first step. Concentrate on what you are doing, not on what you are feeling.

→ Practise your assertion skills but recognise that not all situations demand maximum assertion.

→ Learn to say 'No' some of the time.

→ Use time-management techniques but don't expect them to work all the time.

→ Practise using positive self-talk. We can do something about every situation that causes us stress.

→ Get the balance in life right. No one on their deathbed wishes they had spent more time in the office.

→ Retain a sense of humour. Above all, laugh at yourself and the predicaments that you land yourself in.

Source: adapted from a lecture by Dr John Edmondson

## In practice...

*Ernie, a very successful senior civil servant, went out one lunch time to get some money from the cash machine. After three failed attempts at his PIN the bank machine retained his card. He told me that he began to shake and almost cried. At that point he realised that he was seriously stressed and could not continue to work in the same way.*

*He returned to his office, cleared his diary for the afternoon and went for a long walk. He decided to stop taking a briefcase to work as that way he wouldn't carry unread documents back and forth and worry about not reading them all the time. He joined the golf club and plays every Saturday morning. At work he put 30 minutes' preparation and 15 minutes' debrief time in his diary around every meeting. Ernie successfully recognised and dealt with his own stress problem.*

## Read around

*Managing your mind*, G. Butler and T. Hope

*The good stress guide*, M. Hartley

## Links to other leadership tips

**36**  Recharge your batteries

**65**  Spend your time wisely as a leader

**95**  Generate fun at work

# Recognise that your habitual leadership STYLE is ineffective or becoming stale

*Consistency is contrary to nature. The only truly consistent people are dead.*

Aldous Huxley, author

Whether you have are an experienced leader or this is your first leadership job, from time to time you will notice that it seems harder to get the work done, new ideas have dried up or perhaps people just don't seem quite as enthusiastic as they were. Or perhaps you need to launch a big new initiative and are worried that the team might not react positively to it. Or even that it is hard to raise the enthusiasm to get up for work in the morning.

These can all be signs that you should stop and think about your leadership style and what changes you might need to make to re-awaken your interest and re-inspire your team.

→ Begin by listing what is going well; be honest and specific. Then ask yourself when you last praised individuals for these achievements or walked the job. If it has been a while, you have identified your first actions.

→ Next list the problems as you see them. Avoid generalisations such as 'people are not getting on with the job'. Ask yourself instead, 'What is it that I expect to see?'; 'What is not happening?'; 'Who is not delivering? On what task? When? How often?' and so on until you have a clear picture. Ask yourself when you last discussed these with your managers or your team. There may be another action here.

→ Find someone to give you honest and accurate feedback about how the team is feeling and what it sees as the problem with your style. Or invest in a confidential, facilitated 360-degree feedback exercise. Accept the feedback, don't justify or defend your actions. Then think about what you need to do to act on it.

→ Think about the personalities of the people in your team and, using the model in chapter 6 to identify the most important things you need to do to improve the relationship with each of them. Then take action as soon as you can.

→ Get yourself a coach or a mentor with whom you can discuss your concerns in confidence and who will help you to clarify your thinking and identify your most successful options.

→ If you genuinely believe that you have outgrown the job or that you are no longer committed to it, move on.

## In practice...

*Clive Woodward spent part of his working life in Australia where he was employed by Rank Xerox as a sales manager.*

*He says in his autobiography: 'I learnt a hard lesson. It is important to study the culture of a country, company, or even a sports team, before barging in. I had wrongly assumed that the culture of Rank Xerox in the UK was worldwide. Clearly it was not ... it was very different in Australia. What worked well for me in the UK did not work at all down under.*

*'I did not make that mistake again with the England Rugby Football Elite squad'.*

## Read around

*Winning*, Sir Clive Woodward

## Links to other leadership tips

# Leadership tip **64**
# Pick and nurture your SUCCESSOR

Research among America's Fortune 500 companies by Jim Collins, and reported in his book *Good to great*, demonstrated a very strong positive link between the long-term success of an organisation and the appointment of a 'home-grown' CEO. So identifying in-house talent and nurturing potential high flyers makes sound business sense.

*Be a gardener at work, grow people.*

Julia Cleverden, CEO, Business in the Community

Talent does not however mean 'someone who reminds me of me'. Picking potential stars on that basis is likely to lead you, and the organisation, into difficulties with equal opportunities and anti-discrimination legislation, and possibly with staff organisations. It will also limit the organisation's ability to change and seize new opportunities and different ways of working. This is likely to be even more disastrous in the long term.

The only safe way to identify and nurture talent is to provide opportunities for leaders to move around the organisation to gain experience in different scenarios. Small organisations may have fewer possibilities of doing this so should consider the possibilities of short-term secondments or attachments to provide additional development opportunities.

Be clear about the skills and behaviours *necessary* and those that are *desirable* for the leadership job. Ensure that you provide opportunities to develop the necessary skills and behaviours. Live with the absence of others – they will be compensated for by other traits you hadn't expected.

Give accurate, honest and timely feedback.

Deliver on your promises. Remember that most new recruits are highly motivated and want to make a success of the job. If they become de-motivated it is because the organisation has de-motivated them.

Your successor will have two main characteristics:

→ She will take over when you go on holiday and you will return to calm effectiveness.

→ He will generate future-focused ideas based on improving client service and growing the operation.

Once you have identified and developed your successor – resign. It is time to move on.

## In practice...

*'Ten out of eleven good-to-great CEOs came from inside the company, three of them by family inheritance. The comparison companies turned to outsiders with six times greater frequency – yet they failed to produce sustained great results.'*

Source: J. Collins, *Good to great*

## Read around

*Good to great*, J. Collins

## Links to other leadership tips

**25** Embed new behaviours in line with the values in your organisation

**39** Use business performance coaching

**75** Develop self-esteem in others

# Leadership tip **65**

# Spend your TIME wisely as a leader

*There is more to life
than increasing its
speed.*

Mahatma Ghandi,
lawyer, politician

The biggest challenge of leadership is to be accountable for things you have to trust other people to do without knowing the details of what they are up to. The temptation is always to check up frequently, create endless 'don't forget' lists and fill your days with progress meetings – all of which get in the way of actual progress being made.

Good leaders know the difference between their role and their accountabilities and spend their time on the former. They have excellent information systems which tell them how well the organisation is doing and enable them to ask occasional searching questions which make others think 'I wish I'd thought of that'. They always have time for individuals and are genuinely interested in their people.

You will be spending your time wisely when you have asked and answered the following questions:

→ What is the particular value I add to the organisation in this role?

→ Do I spend time developing the key relationships which the organisation relies on me to establish and maintain – upwards, downwards and outwards?

→ Am I walking the job and communicating regularly?

→ Do I take time out regularly to think about the future of the organisation, keep up to date with developments in the sector and in the professional community?

→ Am I developing myself? Am I confident in modern IT, financial and statistical techniques, and management and leadership thinking?

→ What do I spend my time on during the day/week/ month? (You may need to keep a record for a while before you can answer this and you will probably be surprised at what you discover.)

→ Am I spending my time on my role or on reaching downwards? Do I delegate effectively, especially things I like doing but which are really appropriate to more junior staff? (We all tend to hang onto a few such tasks because they provide some comfort when facing a bigger job.)

→ Do I distinguish between what is urgent and what is important? By concentrating on what is important I prevent things becoming urgent and can find ways to prevent problems becoming crises (see the model opposite).

→ Do I know when and how to say 'No'?

→ When I am very busy am I sure that this is the best use of my time?

→ Do I know what I want to have achieved in five years' time?

## Task prioritisation

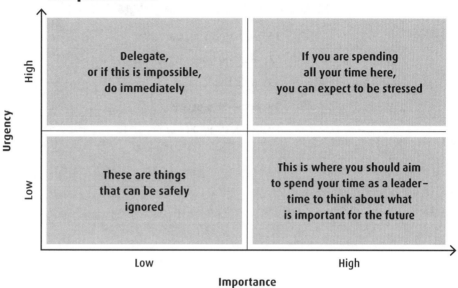

### In practice...

*The job of a leader is to do with people. The job of a manager is to do with things. Both jobs can be categorised into issues that are important or unimportant. They can also be categorised into those items that are urgent and those that are not. The secret of success in both areas is to concentrate on things which are important before they become urgent.*

*Brian used to leave the purchase of his wife's birthday and Christmas presents until the last minute, with the usual disappointing results. He now maintains a list of potential gifts throughout the year and purchases items off this list as and when he sees them. In this way, present-buying for a loved one, which is in the important category, never hits the urgent category.*

## Read around

*First things first*, S. Covey and A. Merrill

*The seven habits of highly effective people*, S. Covey

## Links to other leadership tips

# Leadership tip **66**
# **Prepare for TOP positions**

There are very few short cuts to the top. To get there requires hard work over the long haul. To survive this journey we need continuous good health, lots of common sense, very broad shoulders, a high stress tolerance and a stable private life. In addition, the development or acquisition of the following leadership attributes during the period of preparation will serve you well when you achieve your ambition.

*The harder I practise the luckier I get.*

Tony Jacklin, golfer

→ An ability to act and look the part of a senior executive.

→ Having new, creative and different ways of solving problems.

→ A recognition of the time to seize opportunities.

→ Constant adaptability and the ability to improvise.

→ A positive attitude to change from wherever it comes.

→ A willingness to learn and try new and different approaches.

→ Conscious identification and development of the skills or experience lacking in your curriculum vitae.

→ A real consideration of the needs of others including those from other walks of life.

→ The moral courage to take the really tough decisions.

→ Dedication to the organisation as a whole as well as to your own team.

→ A willingness to delegate as much as possible, particularly the things that you like doing.

→ Communication in all its forms – upwards, downwards, sideways and to the media.

→ Positioning your approach so that you do not spring big surprises on any stakeholder.

→ An ability to pick winners to champion and promote.

→ The courage to appoint people who will usurp you eventually.

Source: adapted from Sir Peter White, *Preparing for the top*

### In practice...

*From the time he left university at the age of 21, Jim committed him-self to becoming a CEO. His plan involved working as an employee for three specified companies within his chosen field for significant but relatively short periods. He made sure that he had a knowledge of the latest business and financial techniques and the latest IT and business modelling tools and that he had done his MBA.*

*He emerged as a chief executive at the age of 32.*

### Read around

*Preparing for the top*, Admiral Sir Peter White

### Links to other leadership tips

**37** Influence your boss

**43** Write and implement your own leadership development plan

**99** Think strategically

Leadership tip **67**

# Develop and maintain TRUST

Trust cannot be gained by demand. 'You'll just have to trust me on this' is often a weak excuse by a manager who either does not know the answer or is unwilling to share the information. In either case the statement is most likely to have the opposite effect – to make listeners even more sceptical.

The extent to which trust is maintained and grows is dependent on how the leader behaves all the time.

Trust is like a deposit account – everything you do and say either adds to or reduces it. There are no exceptions, even when you are having a bad day.

Some people are willing to trust a leader from the outset, expecting the best. They can be a real support and a source of quick feedback. They tend to have deeply held beliefs and convictions and, if the leader does or says something that loses their trust, they can become extremely critical, taking a very long time to begin to trust him or her again.

At the other extreme are those who are sceptical of the leader's trustworthiness from the outset. They can generally be won over gradually, once they have satisfied themselves that based on their own experience they are unlikely to be let down. Any setback will result in almost irreparable harm to the relationship.

Most people will give you the benefit of the doubt unless and until you lose their trust.

The difficulty is that we all use different trust currencies and unless the leader is using the correct one there is no deposit.

Magicians will build trust on being given free rein and having their ideas respected. Lovers build trust on having their feelings considered and the feelings and reactions of others taken into account. Warriors build trust on having clear goals and being rewarded for achieving them. Sovereigns build trust by being consulted and seeing things happen according to the agreed rules.

*A man who doesn't trust himself can never trust anyone else.*

Cardinal de Retz, philosopher and republican

Whatever the personality of your people you will build trust with them by:

→ being open and honest;

→ treating everyone fairly;

→ doing what you say, when you promised;

→ admitting your mistakes;

→ accepting your responsibilities;

→ trusting them;

→ trusting yourself.

Source: adapted from S. Covey, *The seven habits of highly effective people*

## *In practice...*

*Sheridan is Margaret's business partner. When she was ill in 2004, with-out being asked he took over her business responsibilities and tasks, spoke to clients and kept her part of the business running for her.*

*Integrity builds trust. By doing the things that have to be done to the standard needed and the timescale required trust is established.*

## *Read around*

*The seven habits of highly effective people*, S. Covey

## *Links to other leadership tips*

**30** Recognise and motivate a magician

**31** Recognise and motivate a lover

**32** Recognise and motivate a warrior

**33** Recognise and motivate a sovereign

# Leadership tip **68**
# Take **UNPOPULAR DECISIONS**

Anyone can make the easy decisions that everyone will agree with. It is taking the tough decisions, which are for the overall good but will cause hardship or inconvenience to some, that distinguish the leader from the manager.

The 'right' answer is not simply the compromise. Compromising when your gut is telling you to stick to your judgement will not serve the organisation well.

Before taking a difficult decision consider the following five steps, known as 'The Five Cs'.

## 1 Consider the objectives

→ What is the decision intended to achieve?

→ By when must the decision be taken?

→ What are the constraints involved?

→ What would be the effect if no decision were taken?

→ What information is needed?

→ Who should take the decision?

## 2 Consult those affected

→ Have all the people who should be consulted been identified?

→ Have you met with consultative committees and trade union representatives?

→ Has a date been set for the conclusion of the process?

→ Have you attempted to use creative techniques such as brainstorming?

→ Are you prepared to listen to suggestions without jumping to conclusions?

→ Recognise that consultation is not negotiation.

## 3 Commit to making up your mind

→ Review your objectives. Classify them into 'must achieve' and 'would like to achieve'.

*If after consultation, you think 'X' and they think 'Y', the answer is not 'Y' or 'X+Y' divided by two. The answer is 'X'.*

John Garnett, Director, The Industrial Society, 1962–86

→ List all options; evaluate options against objectives.

→ Choose the best option and assess the consequences.

→ Take the decision with commitment and enthusiasm.

**4 Communicate**

→ Have all of those affected been briefed, with reasons?

→ Are the channels for feedback fully understood?

**5 Check the implementation by walking the job**

→ Is corrective action necessary?

→ Have people understood the implications of the decision?

→ Are standards being achieved or can quality be improved further?

→ Can authority be delegated for subsequent decisions?

Source: J. Garnett, *The work challenge*

## *In practice...*

*Margaret was responsible for implementing a peer review process that was very unwelcome to senior staff. They attacked her personally and professionally and sought to undermine her credibility in order to get their own way.*

*Because Margaret had prepared the ground well by working through the above stages and in particular had consulted widely, she succeeded despite the opposition.*

## *Read around*

*Feel the fear and do it anyway,* S. Jeffers

*The work challenge,* J. Garnett

## *Links to other leadership tips*

**35** Analyse problems

**69** Walk the job

**72** Consult those affected before making a decision

# Leadership tip **69**
## WALK the job

At its simplest, walking the job describes the actions of leaders who get out and about around the organisation and listen to their staff. It has enormous benefits as the TV documentary 'Back to the floor' demonstrated – direct feedback, increased understanding and faster problem solving.

Walking the job requires effort and real commitment. It is not always easy to find time to visit the far-flung reaches of the operation – or even the post room. You will need to be realistic about the time you can make available and be ruthless about protecting it.

Many leaders feel very uncomfortable about walking around, feeling that they should have something specific to discuss before appearing. Leaders who only appear when they want something done do not encourage their staff to be open with them about how the organisation is progressing. On the other hand, using the need to give positive feedback and praise as an opportunity to walk around begins the conversation on a positive note.

*We are not born with maps; we have to make them, and the making requires effort. The more effort we make to appreciate and perceive reality, the larger and more accurate our maps will be.*

M. Scott Peck, author

### *In practice...*

*In his early working life Brian had a boss who knew that he was supposed to walk the job and yet he did not know how to do it. He would walk into the room in which the team was working and look at the lights in the ceiling. After a few desultory remarks he would depart – leaving them with a feeling of 'What was all that about?'.*

*He looked at the lights so often that they used to call him 'the electrician'.*

There are some simple guidelines to help you make the most of the time you spend:

→ Vary your route and your timing; don't just go to places where you get a good reception or forget the night shift.

→ Be honest about why you are there, 'I just wanted to hear how things are going', 'I have some good news about the order so I thought I'd come along and tell you and hear what you think about the new initiative'.

→ Avoid the 'Stand by your beds' syndrome, sit where possible and talk to individuals or small groups. Tell people to gather round if at all possible.

→ Look, question and listen, don't just talk. People will usually be delighted to explain their specialism to you and will be happy talking about their job.

→ Talk about their jobs and their concerns, not yours.

→ You will gather suggestions as you go. It is important to explain that you will be discussing them with the managers and that it will be the managers who will be conveying the responses. Doing this ensures that you keep your managers informed and that they don't feel left out or undermined.

→ Say thanks as you leave.

## Read around

*The work challenge*, J. Garnett

## Links to other leadership tips

# Chapter 8
# Achieving extraordinary results as a team leader

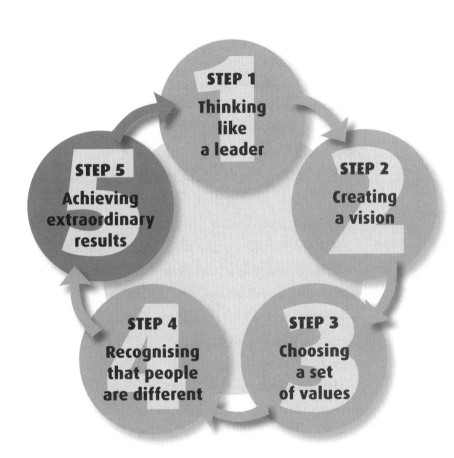

# Leadership tip **70**
## Resolve a 'BREAKDOWN'

A 'breakdown' arises when someone can no longer see the possibility of achieving an objective due to a real or perceived obstacle. Breakdowns are too often left unattended. After all, every breakdown is an opportunity to make a breakthrough for the team and for the organisation. The technique outlined below is a way of resolving difficulties objectively and can prevent harmful interpretations blocking progress.

→ Declare the breakdown.

→ Identify who is affected by it.

→ Put it on the table with a commitment to getting it resolved.

→ Explore the breakdown.

→ Look at key concerns:

   → Why do you care about resolving this breakdown?

   → What are the central causes of the breakdown?

   → Which assessments of damage should we focus our attention on?

   → What real-life examples support these assessments?

   → What standards do we have, and do we agree with them?

→ Reconfirm and re-interpret the problem

→ Move the breakdown to resolution:

   → Speculate on a solution.

   → Make tentative suggestions.

   → Formulate actions.

→ Actions involve someone making a request to do things differently or someone else making a promise to do things differently.

→ A request must be 'SMART' – specific, measurable, action orientated and time bound.

*We've just had a breakdown – how fascinating!*

Ben Zander, conductor, author

→ There are three possible responses to a SMART request:

  → 'Yes, I accept. I promise to deliver X by Y to Z standards.'

  → 'No, I decline.' (For 'Yes' to exist, the possibility of 'No' must also exist.)

  → A commitment to negotiate the SMART terms attached to the request – 'I commit to commit later' or 'My counter offer is…'.

→ What can we learn from this that will help us in the future?

→ How can we prevent it happening again?

## In practice...

*Billy, the marketing director, had the responsibility for ordering 10,000 company Christmas cards. This he did using a charity. Due to a misunderstanding, when the cards arrived the company logo was far too big. The charity did not have the resources to reprint them in time.*

*Billy found that the hard bit was going to his boss to declare the breakdown. Once this was done the relief was enormous. He and his boss agreed that the cards as printed would not do, that they would take no action against the charity and that Billy had to find a commercial organisation to get a reprint done within four working days.*

## Read around

*The art of possibility*, B. Zander

## Links to other leadership tips

**35**  Analyse problems

**80**  Question others

## Leadership tip **71**

# COMMUNICATE OPENLY

Communication is the exchange of information, views, ideas or feelings between two or more people. When achieved, it results in understanding arising from the two-way process of speaking and listening.

Full and open communication means being willing to share enough of oneself so that others recognise the essential person. It is the first step in building trust. It ensures that accurate information flows freely to and from the people who can benefit from it, enabling them to make better decisions and generate new initiatives, links and ideas, creating opportunities for themselves and the business.

*And once sent out a word takes wing irrevocably.*

Horace, philosopher

It is the responsibility of a good leader to inform staff fully of all decisions that affect them, to ensure that they are consulted effectively and at the earliest possible time and to explain the reasons behind changed thinking. A leader freely gives people all the information possible so staff know what is going on and feel part of the corporate family, carrying out their responsibilities with enhanced commitment.

There will be circumstances when you cannot communicate everything that you know, for example, during negotiations about a major reorganisation or a takeover. In those circumstances, a good leader will answer a request for information by saying 'I cannot inform you at present, but as soon as I can, I will'.

No one communication method can achieve all these objectives nor is one method appropriate for all types of message.

Research shows that when information affects someone personally, for instance redundancy or a major change to their job, communication is most effective when they hear it first from a trusted manager, face to face. The less immediate the effect on the individual the more effective general communications can be, for instance e-mails, memos, newsletters and websites.

So to communicate effectively in an organisation, a combination of approaches is required; plus a willingness to be open, honest and trusting in all dealings with people.

|  | Specific info | General info |
|---|---|---|
| **...that affects me** | **Walking the job**<br>**One-to-one meetings**<br>**Open and honest feedback**<br>**Progress reports**<br>**Instructions, orders** | **Walking the job**<br>**Team meetings**<br>**Brainstorming**<br>**Away days** |
| **...that affects everyone** | **Disciplinary procedure**<br>**Grievance procedure**<br>**Newsletters**<br>**Memos, circulars** | **Consultative meetings**<br>**Culture/attitude surveys**<br>**Inter and intranet sites**<br>**Open line sessions** |

## *In practice...*

*Effective communication is often short, heartfelt and redolent with feelings:*

*'Our deepest fear is not that we are inadequate.*
*Our deepest fear is that we are powerful beyond measure.*
*It is our light, not our darkness that most frightens us.*
*We ask ourselves, "who am I to be brilliant, gorgeous, talented, fabulous?"*
*Actually, who are you not to be?*
*You are a child of God.*
*Your playing small doesn't serve the world.*
*There's nothing enlightened about shrinking so that other people don't feel insecure around you.*
*We are all meant to shine as children do.*
*We are born to manifest the glory of God that is within us.*
*It's not just in some of us; it's in everyone.*
*And as we let our own light shine, we unconsciously give other people permission to do the same.*
*As we are liberated from our fear, our presence automatically liberates others.'*

Source: Marianne Williamson, poet quoted by
Nelson Mandela in his inaugural speech

## Read around

*Peak performance presentations,* R. Olivier and N. Janni

## Links to other leadership tips

# CONSULT those affected before making a decision

When consultation has taken place, cooperation and commitment are far more likely to exist. The most effective way of involving people is to adopt the approach of 'consultation before decision'. Consulting people after a decision is rarely productive and frequently leads to resentment.

If there is no possibility of changing the decision, don't consult about it. If appropriate, do consult about the best means of implementation. Be clear.

Consultation is necessary because people perceive opportunities, benefits, facts and situations from different standpoints. Their feelings are involved, their interests affected, their jobs and security may be threatened and, above all, they often have the knowledge and experience that springs from having to carry out decisions and doing the actual work. Others have much to contribute to the decision-making process. A leader consults to get the best decision and then takes the decision personally.

*After all the voices have been heard and the decision made the rule is – 'Everyone has to adhere to the decision and support it in public… or resign'.*

William Rodgers, former US Secretary of State

## Timescales

There is usually a strong case for consulting as early as practicable, so as to allow as much time as possible to weigh up the pros and cons of the situation. This has to be measured against the need to avoid long drawn-out discussions of contentious issues, as well as avoiding raising hopes or apprehensions unnecessarily early.

## Checklist

→ Have all the people who should be consulted been identified including those affected in other departments and locations?

→ Has the information, including the constraints, been assembled?

→ Have meetings been convened with consultative committees and trade union representatives?

→ Has the timing been carefully chosen and a date set for the conclusion of the process?

→ Have you attempted to think outside the problem by creating a task force and using creative techniques such as brainstorming?

→ Are you fully prepared to listen to ideas and suggestions without jumping to conclusions?

→ Beware of the downside of a compromise decision. Consultation is not negotiation.

→ Be prepared to explain and defend your decision.

## *In practice...*

*George was a senior manager in the City of London. His department occupied office space that was costing the company £66 per square foot per annum which was some of the most expensive office space in London at the time. There was a need to cut costs.*

*George openly consulted the staff without having made his mind up as to the possible solutions. The staff agreed that they would cut the amount of filing in half so George arranged a filing party – orange juice, cakes and plastic bin bags. Unwanted files went into the bags, wanted files were archived. The reduction in filing space was 50% and the rental saving was in excess of £40,000 per year.*

## *Read around*

*The last word on power*, T. Goss

## *Links to other leadership tips*

# Leadership tip **73**

## Create and use CRITICAL FRIENDS

All leaders enter a period when success begins to appear habitual. And it is the string of successes can lead to the leader's downfall. They begin to think that they can do no wrong and that everything they touch will turn to gold. It is at times like these when critical friends are needed.

Critical friends are trusted individuals who are prepared to tell the leader where they are going wrong.

As with all friendship, the basis of critical friendship at work is shared values and open and honest communication. These relationships will enable personal trust to be established between the leader and follower.

It may be difficult for the leader to hear and take notice of unpalatable truths, so he or she needs to receive the message constructively and take care not to 'bite the messenger'.

Followers may find the task of informing their boss that they have made a big mistake daunting. This can take courage. The leader needs to establish an atmosphere at work whereby constructive criticism is encouraged and not taken personally. In turn, this can only be achieved when trust exists.

When receiving the advice of critical friends:

→ Acknowledge the criticism and thank them for it.

→ If you can take action immediately, do so. This will build credibility and encourage others to do the same.

→ If you cannot take action immediately, promise your critical friend that you will think deeply about the issue and give them a time when you will give them your decision.

→ Stick to this time frame.

→ If you decide not to take the advice, give your reasons and tell them to keep thinking about what is happening and to keep bringing things to you.

'No-men' are the most precious of followers and 'yes-men' the most lethal. It is followers who make leaders and it is followers with a strength of belief in what is right who can save leaders from failure.

## In practice...

*The key advantage that the Allied leaders had over Hitler was that each had a constructive dissenter prepared to tell them, when the right time came, that what they were intending to do was wrong. Roosevelt had Marshall, Stalin had Antonov and Churchill had Brooke.*

*Hitler had only 'yes-men' and as a result made appalling blunders, such as the winter invasion of the Soviet Union.*

## Read around

*Elizabeth 1 CEO*, A. Axelrod

## Links to other leadership tips

**12** Create a vision for your own operation

**18** Decide your own set of values

**53** Really listen

**67** Develop and maintain trust

# Leadership tip **74**
# DELEGATE responsibly

The dictionary defines delegating as committing power to an agent or deputy, entrusting a task to another and sending or authorising a person as a representative. That is a far cry for dumping stuff you don't want to do on whoever happens to be nearest – the behaviour which has earned delegation a bad name among many people. At its best true delegation has several major advantages. It ensures that:

→ Leaders are spending their time wisely on important issues that merit their attention.

→ Staff are being developed and grown in their jobs by being given opportunities to learn new skills.

→ Work is being carried out at the lowest safe level in the organisation and decisions are being made closer to the real action thereby reducing costs and likelihood of error.

*Here lies a man who knew how to enlist in his services better men than himself.*

Self-chosen epitaph of Andrew Carnegie, industrialist

To delegate well, you as a leader must give up the satisfaction of doing some of the things you do normally, some of the things that keep you in control and some of the things that you enjoy doing. The benefits include more time to think and contribute at your senior level, the satisfaction of developing others and building increased capacity in the organisation.

Many leaders baulk at the idea of delegating tasks they enjoy, suggesting that they need to keep some 'nice' things in the in-box. Bear in mind that in general we all enjoy doing things we are good at. And we became good at them through practice. Someone once gave us a chance to begin to learn, so if we have done something for a long time isn't it time we too gave someone else a chance? If we spend the time saved on things we find difficult now, in time we will begin to enjoy them too.

All delegation involves some risk. Minimise this by careful planning, good communication and by showing people that you, as a leader, have faith in their ability. Remain interested and coach those new to the task.

**Always:**

→ Assess who could do the task and what training or development they might need before you delegate. Discuss this with them. Take time to coach and support, remain interested but do not take over.

→ Delegate the necessary authority with the responsibility; tell those who need to know that Susie will be acting for you.

225

→ Recognise that you, as a leader, retain the public accountability if things do go wrong. Do not let this stop you.

**Never:**

→ Delegate to a group of people or a team; always delegate to an individual.

→ Abdicate responsibility for confidential, security or policy matters restricted to your level.

→ Use delegation to 'set someone up' or prove a point; people will not trust you again.

## In practice...

*Fiona was responsible for the development and introduction of a new £6 million IT programme. This needed a large team of skilled professionals and a team leader with excellent interpersonal skills. Fiona carefully recruited the team and chose Ted as team leader because of his ability to lead people. She spent several days explaining the origins of the project to Ted, the outcomes and benefits of success, and introducing him to all the key stakeholders.*

*Thereafter she brought the team together, outlined the vision and the key deliverables, and left the meeting.*

*Ted came to see her several hours later with a detailed programme plan which the team had created. The programme took 18 months to implement and throughout Fiona felt as if she was sitting on her hands on top of an active volcano – championing the work at senior meetings and remaining accountable for it while keeping out of the day-to-day detail.*

*This delegation worked; and Ted and the team delivered the major IT programme on budget and on time.*

## Read around

*Elizabeth 1 CEO*, A. Axelrod

## Links to other leadership tips

Leadership tip **75**

# Develop self-ESTEEM in others

Leadership is the art of action at a distance. Organisations are made great by their people and it is the leader's job to keep them committed, enthusiastic and effective at work. The key to this is developing their self-esteem – their sense of self-worth, being valued and being successful. You must demonstrate your belief in them all the time.

## Build relationships

→ Get to know your people as individuals, not just job descriptions, understand their hopes and aspirations.

→ Trust people and promote an environment of trust between all individuals and teams.

→ Listen.

→ Be generous. Share your own knowledge, skills and expertise.

## Be clear and enthusiastic

→ Provide a clear and unchanging vision for your part of the organisation.

→ Translate this into a mission and then into goals with strategies and milestones.

→ Agree targets and parameters with individuals and the team as a whole.

→ Put requests across with enthusiasm and conviction.

→ Demonstrate your belief in everything you do by living the vision – if you don't mean it, don't say it and expect others to believe you.

## Be honest

→ Act with sincerity, openness and fairness to all.

→ Provide praise when it is deserved and celebrate successes with teams and individuals.

→ Give accurate and timely feedback – good and bad.

→ Demonstrate that you are prepared to 'fight the corner' of your people, when appropriate.

→ Acknowledge difficulties and involve them in finding solutions.

*Treat people as if they were what they ought to be and you help them to become what they are capable of being.*

Goethe, poet

**Build ownership**

→ Permit easy access to as much information as possible.

→ Ensure individuals have authority to make the necessary decisions.

→ Ask for the opinions of others and listen to the responses.

→ Allow people the time to resolve their own problems.

→ Promote wide-ranging development opportunities.

→ When possible act as coach.

→ Raise the profile of individuals and the team by encouraging public recognition and praise for their achievements.

## *In practice...*

*Julie was the CEO of a small charity. Both she and her team of professional managers were demoralised and under pressure from the trustees to take action and produce results which they privately thought were impossible.*

*In order to overcome this lack of self-esteem in the team, Julie arranged a workshop. She asked the team members to forget about the current uncomfortable situation in which they found themselves. She asked them to take themselves back into the past and express the real reasons why they had decided to join this voluntary organisation. She listed these reasons and asked them all to keep them at the forefront of their minds.*

*She them asked, 'If you had a magic wand, what would you now do with this organisation of ours?'. This produced a long list of suggestions, some of which could be actioned quickly. These 'quick fixes' lifted morale, built self-esteem and enabled the team to take action in areas which had previously seemed impossible.*

## *Read around*

*How to win friends and influence people,* D. Carnegie

## *Links to other leadership tips*

**1** Begin to think like a leader

**9** Use the dyadic or relationship-based approach

**47** Build your self-esteem without becoming arrogant

**74** Delegate responsibly

# Leadership tip **76**
# Give and receive FEEDBACK

The purpose of feedback is to help a person, or a team, to perceive the effect of their behaviour. It enables them to make decisions about their own future behavioural changes.

There is a three-step approach to giving feedback:

**1** What I thought you did well…

**2** What I thought you did less well…

**3** My suggestions for future improvements are…

Avoid linking 1 and 2 with 'but', 'though' or 'however'. Such linking words destroy the impact of the positive feedback.

*Feedback is a mirror which I can use to help me to see how I appear to others and the impact my behaviour is having on them. It enables me to identify facets of my behaviour, which I may choose to change.*

Anne Stratton, trainer

| When giving feedback: | When receiving feedback: |
|---|---|
| Get permission to give feedback | Really listen |
| Be clear for whose benefit this is | Try not to be defensive |
| Get your time and place right, as soon after the event as is sensitively possible | Don't interrupt or justify |
| Be specific, use facts and examples. If you are using opinions state them as opinions | Encourage the other to be forthright and honest |
| State why you are giving this feedback | Accept the feedback |
| Focus on do-able changes | Thank the giver of the feedback |
| Balance positives and negatives | Remember that feedback is only one opinion and that nothing has to be changed as a result |
| Focus on behaviour not personality | Act on the feedback if you believe it will make a difference |
| Check that your feedback has been received in the way it was intended | Tell the feedback giver what you are going to do, if anything |

## In practice...

*A friend of ours, an experienced public speaker, used to start her session on giving and receiving feedback by saying:*

*'I am prepared to take feedback from anyone at any time apart from:*
*– my mother*
*– my partner*
*– my boss*
*– my work colleagues and*
*– my peer group.'*

*The implication being that we are all more ready to receive feedback from strangers than we are from those closest to us.*

*It is those closest to us who can provide the most revealing insights provided we are prepared to treat them as critical friends.*

## Links to other leadership tips

**53**  Really listen

**73**  Create and use critical friends

Leadership tip **77**

# Lead when the FOLLOWERS won't follow

When things go wrong, it is only natural for a leader to want to blame the followers. Ghengis Khan used to wield the sword to take the heads off followers who refused to follow. Today we may not be able to wield a literal sword but many of us have wished for an imaginary one with which to shout, to scream, to sack individuals, to discipline staff.

This tendency should be resisted. History is full of examples of leaders who wanted it all their own way and caused the followers to rebel. The Caine Mutiny and the Gunpowder Plot are both cases in point. The major issue is to take personal responsibility for the failure and ask oneself some searching questions.

**What kind of failure was this?**

### 1. A failure of vision or values

→ Was the vision too limited to motivate people to do great things?

→ Was the vision superseded by a better idea emanating from outside the organisation?

→ Was the vision too grand and therefore unachievable?

→ Did you make the vision real for your followers?

→ Were your values aligned with theirs?

### 2. A failure of mission

→ Was the plan good enough and the resources sufficient for the task?

→ Were the communication links inside and outside the organisation good enough to appreciate the larger picture?

### 3. A failure of execution

→ Was the work carefully designed?

→ Were the skills of the people right for the task?

→ Was the group properly trained?

If the answer to any of the above is 'No', then you have the makings of the beginnings of failure. If the answer is 'Yes' to all of the above, proceed to the next question.

**Was it something in me that caused the failure?**

→ Did I fail to recognise that things had changed soon enough?

→ Did I put too much emphasis on the trappings of leadership and not enough on the responsibilities of leadership and good relationships with others?

→ Did I lead in everything I did?

→ What can I learn from this failure that will prevent me from making the same mistakes again?

## In practice...

*Ron was the captain of his cricket team. Without consulting his team mates he went out to toss the coin with the opposition skipper. The toss of the coin determines which side will bat and which will bowl. Ron won the toss and elected to bat in conditions most helpful to the opposition bowlers.*

*Ron's team was dismissed for a very low score.*

*In the dressing room at the tea break mutiny erupted and the team refused to take the field, criticising Ron's poor leadership and bad decision-making. Ron asked for two minutes' silence and then said, 'I am sorry. I made a mistake this afternoon. I won't make the same mistake in the future without consulting you. I ask you please will you help me reverse the effects of my poor decision.'*

*The team went out with enthusiasm and won the game.*

## Read around

*South, the endurance expedition*, E. Shackleton

## Links to other leadership tips

**4** Tell the difference between management and leadership

**12** Create a vision for your own operation

**18** Decide your own set of values

**21** Tell when it is time to resign

**82** Reduce resistance to your leadership initiative

# Leadership tip 78
## Conduct a values-based MEETING

Values-based meetings are held within a code of conduct that is founded on the organisation's values. All those at the meeting agree to adhere to these 'ground rules'.

As well as the usual duties, the person chairing a values-based meeting has two additional responsibilities:

→ Remind the meeting of the agreed ground rules at the outset.

→ Challenge behaviour and comments during the discussion that are outside the rules.

Each organisation has its own values, whether or not these are explicit. When drawing up the ground rules for the first time it is important to take each value in turn and ask what it means for the meeting and discussion.

### Some examples of commonly used ground rules

For holding meetings:

→ Meetings do not begin before 08.30 or after 16.30.

→ Meetings begin and end on time.

→ People arrive on time.

→ Necessary information is shared in good time beforehand and necessary preparation done.

→ Minutes/decisions and action summaries are shared afterwards within agreed timescales.

For the discussions at the meeting:

→ Openness, honesty and courtesy – keep an open mind and speak your mind.

→ Everyone is of equal status at the meeting.

→ All contributions should add value – agree or disagree only if it takes the meeting forward.

→ Everyone participates – no one dominates.

→ Freely give of relevant experience.

→ Be active listeners – talking is not learning.

*Begin with the end in mind.*

Stephen Covey, self-development guru, author

→ Respect requests from the leader.

→ Critique ideas and issues, not individuals.

→ There are no stupid questions.

→ Silence means assent.

→ Humour in the appropriate place is a bonus.

Where confidentiality is an issue – for instance during discussions on future staffing – this should be made clear at the outset and agreement sought. Do not keep secrets unless you really must.

The best of these meetings move into flow. Time seems to stand still, conversation is smooth, no one feels left out, everyone feels they are contributing and the result is new learning as a team.

## In practice...

*A group of professionals from different organisations and back-grounds got together for an open-space discussion about emerging trends in the leadership arena. After an uncomfortable first session the key to subsequent success was the enthusiastic agreement of the behaviours everyone would adhere to.*

*The one dissenting voice decided to leave. Those who had previously been on the sidelines moved to centre stage and the group as a whole quickly moved into flow.*

*The outcome was a model that all present have since used to their advantage in their professional capacities.*

## Read around

*The seven habits of highly effective people*, S. Covey

## Links to other leadership tips

**24**  Create a set of team or organisational values

**85**  Get the best out of teams

**93**  Engage the whole audience

**100** Lead volunteers

## Leadership tip **79**
# Give PRAISE

Psychologists know that healthy humans, both adults and children, need praise in order to develop and grow in confidence. Recently there have been reports of research in America that suggests that people at work get five times less praise than they need.

Think of the last time someone said 'well done' to you. If it was someone whose judgement you respected you probably felt good about the task and about yourself as a result. Merited praise builds self-esteem.

Do not confuse praise with positive feedback.

Praise is statements like 'Well done', 'Great presentation', 'Terrific gift aid figures'; they are judgements which can only be made after something has happened or been completed. They tell you about how the giver evaluated the action but not what made it so good.

Positive feedback provides the information you can use to learn and improve, for example 'You did well to stay calm during that discussion', 'The illustrations made the concept really clear'.

The best praise is from one person to another, face to face. Close second is a handwritten note (not an e-mail). It can be given either privately or in public.

**Always:**

→ Mean it.

→ Be alert to opportunities to give praise whenever and wherever it is deserved – you will not make it meaningless by doing it often. You will only make it meaningless if you are not honest when things have not gone well.

→ Give the praise as soon as it is deserved, don't 'save it for later'.

→ Praise small successes as well as large ones.

→ Praise as many people as possible.

→ Pass on praise from elsewhere and let the person know their work has been noticed, e.g. 'The CEO and several board members have told me how good it was'.

**Never:**

→ Use praise in order to flatter or as a means of trying to get someone to work harder.

→ Praise actions that have called for no particular effort.

→ Debase praise by using it randomly or thoughtlessly.

Remember that praising someone will make you feel good too.

## *In practice...*

*In 1978 trade unions were very powerful.*

*William had delivered a sales skills seminar to an audience that had included John Garnett, who was at the time the CEO of The Industrial Society. The sales presentation had included the golden rule, 'Silence should follow when you have asked for the order'.*

*William received a letter from John Garnett the following week that said:*

> *'Dear William,*
>
> *Thank you for the sales seminar. When arbitrating in the lorry drivers' dispute I made the trade unions an offer and then waited in silence for 11 minutes for their affirmative reply whilst thinking of you and your marvellous advice.*
>
> *Yours John'*

## *Read around*

*The one minute manager,* K. Blanchard and S. Johnson

## *Links to other leadership tips*

**1** Begin to think like a leader

**9** Use the dyadic or relationship-based approach to leadership

**75** Develop self-esteem in others

# Leadership tip **80**
# **QUESTION others**

The ability to ask questions in a way that demonstrates confidence in the other person while gaining the essential information is a key leadership skill.

Questions that focus too narrowly on the task or issue may be heard as aggressive and judgemental. And failure to be clear and direct may equally be seen as lack of understanding and 'pussy-footing'. So choosing the right approach for the issue and the circumstances depends on getting the balance right.

There are two main approaches:

1  **Coaching questions** – to help others explore their understanding, emotions and feelings. This approach is most useful when the key result of the conversation is that the other person learns.

2  **Exploratory questions** – to find out facts and other information. This approach is most useful when the key result of the conversation is that facts or information is established and agreed.

Whichever approach you use, question to learn rather than to blame. Failure to do so will prevent you from getting all the information you need (or think you need).

| Coaching | Question types | Exploratory |
|---|---|---|
| What about this is important to you? | Open | What trends did you extract from this data? |
| How do you feel about this? | Probing | What are the precise numbers for this conclusion? |
| What help do you need? | Closing | Are these figures acceptable to you? |
| How can we conclude this conversation? | Summary | Where does this leave us? |

### *Read around*

*Coaching for performance,* J. Whitmore

*Effective coaching,* M. Downey

### *Links to other leadership tips*

# Leadership tip **81**
## Predict a REACTION to your leadership initiative

There are five different responses you can expect in response to an initiative that you as leader introduce.

They range from involved positivism to covert antagonism, as shown in the model below.

**Evangelists** are people on whom you can not only rely to give you every support in making the initiative work but also to talk positively at every meeting whether you are present or not.

**Enthusiasts** will usually only be enthusiastic in your presence. They will do what you want them to but only what you ask. They will not add value of their own to the initiative.

**Neutral people** will just wait and see which way the wind blows after the initiative has been announced.

**Cynics** want things to stay as they are. They often believe that nothing will happen as they have heard it all before. They will be negative and consider all of the down sides. They will, however, display their negativity to your face.

**Traitors** want an end to your initiative or the end of your leadership role. They are cowards and will never show you their hand, they operate behind your back. They will be negative about the issue to everyone else and they will do everything they can to scupper the proposed course of action.

Source: with acknowledgement to R. Olivier, *Inspirational leadership*

*A cynic is someone who does not wish to be disappointed again.*

Ben Zander, conductor, author

## How will your team react?

First, use the chart below to predict the reaction of each of your team members to the initiative you are proposing.

| Team member | Traitor | Cynic | Neutral | Enthusiast | Evangelist |
|---|---|---|---|---|---|
| A | | | | | |
| B | | Is ———————→ | | Needs to be | |
| C | | | | | |
| D | | | | | |
| E | | | | | |

Secondly, having predicted their reaction, use the chart to indicate how much you have to move their attitudes if the initiative is to be a success.

Thirdly, deal with each group appropriately as follows:

→ Trust and involve the evangelists.

→ Involve and encourage the enthusiasts.

→ Encourage and inform the neutrals.

→ Inform and challenge the cynics.

→ Challenge and, if necessary, sack the traitors.

## *In practice...*

*Kathryn was appointed CEO of an NGO. She was chosen ahead of one internal candidate, Sheila, who remained in her job, reporting to Kathryn.*

*Kathryn believed that Sheila could be won round by open communication, trust and sharing values. On the other hand, Sheila did not believe that Kathryn was worthy of the CEO position.*

*Kathryn spent 18 months trying to encourage, cajole and direct Sheila. She believed that their overarching loyalty to the aims of the organisation would overcome personal differences. However, after 18 months of broken promises, continual failure to deliver and attempts personally to undermine her, Kathryn was faced with the conclusion that Sheila was in fact a traitor.*

*At her appraisal meeting, when Sheila had resorted to tears to excuse the latest round of failings, Kathryn said, 'Sheila, I believe that you could do your job if you wanted to. You must understand that I am not going anywhere so if you want to stay here you will have to get used to that and start working with me'.*

*A month later Sheila had resigned and left the organisation.*

## Read around

*Inspirational leadership*, R. Olivier

*The art of possibility*, B. Zander

## Links to other leadership tips

# Leadership tip **82**
## Reduce RESISTANCE to your leadership initiative

Resistance is a universal reaction to change, particularly from cynics and traitors. To them any change is usually seen as a 'loss' – of influence, personal standing or knowledge of 'how we do things here'. Added to that is the usual human fear of the unknown, so it can be a potent mixture. Moreover, sometimes the stated business reasons for the objections can mask a deeper fear of personal loss.

It is important to be able to distinguish resistance that stems from critical friendship, and which is essential to making consistently good decisions, from the more general resistance to change. The leader's job is to recognise that resistance is a common reaction, to understand the likely impact of the proposed change on individuals and their aspirations, and to build trust and confidence through open and honest communication.

Most individuals see the threat of change as:

→ **Technical** – I will no longer be the expert.

→ **Political** – I will no longer have influence or access.

→ **Organisational** – we shouldn't be doing this, it is too risky.

→ **Personal or individual** – I will be (or will be seen as being) downgraded or I will not be able to handle the new role.

There are some key steps you can take to reduce resistance. However, bear in mind that you will probably not succeed in eliminating it altogether until the change has proved to be a success.

→ Talk about the benefits of the proposed new state of affairs at every opportunity. You will need to devote more time to this than you expect at first and you will find that you have to repeat yourself many times.

→ Listen to the objections raised and respond to them honestly.

→ Consult widely and involve as many people as you can in working out the details.

→ Identify those who are most resistant to the change, understand why they are resisting and identify a strategy to overcome the resistance.

*Leaders are paid for the hard bits, the rest we do for our own amusement.*

Debra Allcock-Tyler
CEO, Directory of Social Change

**Strategies to combat resistance**

| Type of resistance | Underlying issues | Strategy to combat |
|---|---|---|
| Technical | Feelings of inadequacy<br>Fear of looking stupid<br>Lack of information<br>  or skills | Involvement and<br>  information<br>Access to retraining or<br>  additional development<br>Reassurance of value<br>  to the organisation |
| Political | Loss of standing, whether<br>  real or perceived<br>Feeling under-valued | Acknowledge their reason<br>Stress what is gained<br>  rather than what is lost<br>Reassurance of value<br>  to the organisation |
| Organisational | Control<br>Pride<br>Sense of ownership | Listen carefully<br>  to the objection<br>Involve them so that<br>  they feel ownership<br>Modify initiative<br>  if appropriate |
| Personal<br>  or individual | Fear<br>Emotional paralysis | Increase involvement<br>  to decrease fear<br>Reassurance of value<br>  to the organisation<br>Coach into new role |

Source: adapted from G. Eckes, *Making six sigma last*

## Read around

*Making six sigma last*, G. Eckes

## Links to other leadership tips

**53** Really listen

**67** Develop and maintain trust

**72** Consult those affected before making a decision

**81** Predict a reaction to your leadership initiative

**83** Support individuals and teams

**95** Generate fun at work

## Leadership tip **83**
# SUPPORT individuals and teams

An effective leader recognises that there are circumstances where individuals and teams encounter problems that affect their performance, whether these are work-related or personal. When this occurs, help, encouragement and support from the leader can bridge the gap for an individual or a team, until they can overcome their problems.

*I can live for two months on a good compliment.*

Mark Twain, author

As a leader you are going to be expected to be a tower of strength and to lend your support to others who are encountering difficulties either singly or in groups. You can do this in three ways:

**1** You can carry people yourself, in the sense of allowing them to draw emotional, intellectual or physical support from you personally. Take care that you do not allow this to become open ended and turn into permanent dependency. Discuss the difficulty openly and once the acute period has passed, encourage them to take back their responsibility and autonomy in stages.

**2** You can organise your team into a supportive party or network for each other. This involves the team being open and honest with one another and 'rallying round' through the difficulty. Take care that the team does not carry one member indefinitely. If you allow that to happen you will soon find that overall team performance reduces significantly as resentment builds up.

**3** You can encourage your team to provide support outside the team. Lending support beyond the team is a good way of developing leadership skills and attributes in team members and of building effective working relationships across the organisation. It will also enable the team to call on others in times of difficulty or stress.

When supporting individuals or teams there are some key steps for you and the team to take:

→ Really listen.

→ Use open questions to find out the facts.

→ Explore other people's ideas.

→ Build on strengths, address weaknesses.

→ Offer help by adjusting deadlines, suggesting ways of handling unreasonable demands from customers, suppliers and colleagues etc.

→ Demonstrate support with something tangible. The provision of a new piece of equipment or the removal of an obstacle is demonstration of the words, 'I'm with you on this one'.

→ Avoid entering uninvited on personal or emotional issues.

→ Recognise that there is a time to support and a time to challenge, and which is which.

When challenging individuals and teams there are some key steps for you and the team to take:

→ Remind people of the outcomes expected.

→ Tell people the standards you expect.

→ Question others from your perspective.

→ Be open about your feelings.

→ Get people to give of their personal best.

→ Point out when an issue is being avoided.

→ Offer alternative solutions.

## *In practice...*

*John was the creative director of a small print and design firm. His deputy, Mary, missed an important customer deadline and denied responsibility, blaming her team for the problem. John took the necessary steps to deliver the order to the customer and then arranged a private discussion with Mary.*

*He began by reassuring Mary of his high regard for her work generally, reminding her of recent successes. He explained the impact of the missed deadline and asked Mary what support she needed right now. Mary was quiet for some time and then, reluctantly at first, told him about her elderly parents and the illness and disability with which she was struggling. John asked how he or the team could help and Mary suggested that she rearrange her working time and negotiate with the team to provide a rota of cover for some of her supervision tasks. With her permission, John explained the problem to the team and a new work pattern was agreed for the next three months.*

*Once Mary's difficulties were resolved the team decided to retain the rota as team members were enjoying the greater responsibility, so Mary used the additional time to develop a new strand of the business. Everyone gained as a result.*

### Read around

*Emotional intelligence*, D. Goleman

*I'm OK, you're OK*, T. Harris

### Links to other leadership tips

# Leadership tip **84**

# Establish TARGETS with individuals and teams

Targets are almost universally disliked and blamed for stress and 'short-termism' in the workplace. They are often seen as being wholly unrealistic, originating elsewhere and not related to the real activity of the team.

The original purpose of a target was to identify priorities or special tasks that needed to be achieved in addition to normal work. They were about relatively short-term shifts in performance and as such were a helpful addition to standards of performance that were the continuing yardsticks. However nowadays targets are used as the ubiquitous measure of everything. One senior civil servant we know told us that he has 300 targets to meet every year! As a result there are no priorities and no real targets to help shift performance.

Before you start to think about the targets you, as a leader, will set for your team, bear in mind that targets influence behaviour – what you target is what you will get – whether those are the 'right' things for the organisation or not. If the target is 25 calls to possible customers per day, 25 calls will be made. It may be that only one results in a sale but that was not the target so, even if the outcome you needed was to increase sales by 25%, the target has been met and so you may have to reward the performance. That is a common example of 'over-engineering' targets, frequently as a result of lack of trust and micro-management in the organisation.

If a sales director trusts the team, he or she will explain the financial realities, tell everyone that a 25% increase is needed and leave it to the teams to develop strategies to achieve it. On the other hand, lack of trust and a 'command and control' approach would probably result in the sales director calculating the success rate of calls and targeting either an increase in the number of calls or an increase in the number where a sale results. On paper that may seem reasonable. Yet the team may know that different information from other parts of the organisation is what is needed to achieve the increase. Without that knowledge the director will get the targets wrong and the team will be de-motivated as a result.

Targets can be 'hard' or 'soft'. They not only relate to sales or production figures, but also to results that cannot be as easily quantified. Providing both the leader and the individual (or team) understand and agree the intangible nature of the outcome needed, the target – 'improving relationships with another department' – can be as valid a target as 'reducing expenditure by four per cent'.

Targets are best proposed by the team, or the individual, and need to be accompanied by relevant commitments. Targets should be:

→ linked directly to outcomes;

→ kept as clear and simple as possible;

→ agreed at a face-to-face meeting;

→ recorded.

### How many targets?

If more than half a dozen targets are attempted in any one period, in addition to normal work, success in all target areas is unlikely.

### How difficult?

Targets are intended to improve performance and motivate teams and individuals. There is no point in making them too easy. They should be challenging and stretching to give people a real sense of achievement. And at the same time they must be achievable – just.

### Examples of areas for target agreement.

| To | |
|---|---|
| → Innovate | → Develop an individual or team |
| → Rejuvenate a project often set aside | → Cash in on the unexpected |
| → Broaden individual or team skills | → Change priorities in altered circumstances |
| → Guide the high achiever(s) | → Establish a standard of performance |
| → Implement a new policy | → Raise a standard of performance |
| → Develop a new area of work | → Re-establish a slipping standard or target |

## Read around

www.businesslink.gov.uk/settingbusinesstargets

## Links to other leadership tips

# Get the best out of TEAMS

A team is a group of people who are working together for a common purpose. A team differs from a professional association in that the team members communicate openly and rely on one another, thanks to their mutual trust. Good teams are efficient and effective. Great teams are additionally energised and energising, have fun and attract others to them.

Great teams can be said to have six characteristics. They consist of individuals who:

**1** trust one another;

**2** take risks together;

**3** complement each other's strengths;

**4** compensate for each other's weaknesses;

**5** have a common goal or a purpose greater than individual goals;

**6** produce extraordinary results together.

The leader's overriding role is to develop good working relationships with those involved, build trust and keep two-way feedback flowing freely – whether the team is in one room or scattered across the country.

It is the leader's responsibility to ensure that the entire team is enthused by the vision and understands the contribution the team and each individual makes to achieving it.

The key steps to developing a great team are:

→ Encourage the sharing of the team's vision and a set of values.

→ Be willing to engage fully.

→ Set expectations of performance well above current performance.

→ Share the commitment to live up to these expectations.

→ Be willing to model behaviour that lives up to these expectations.

→ Focus on the task and the development of people as well as the organisation as a whole.

→ Care to ask, be interested to listen, and be dedicated enough to respond.

→ Set time aside for one-to-one and team coaching.

→ Share the leadership role and responsibilities while retaining accountabilities.

→ Recognise individual and team success in public.

→ Have the courage to deal with problem team members.

Mediocre teams say 'Our leader holds us accountable'.

Great teams hold themselves mutually accountable.

Source: adapted from T. Goss, *The last word on power*

| How to undertake a high-performance team health check |
| --- |
| Honestly answer the following questions. |
| Score zero in the box on the right of the question if the answer is 'Not at all', two if the answer is 'Somewhat' and five if the answer is 'Totally'. |

| | |
| --- | --- |
| **1** Is there a shared sense of purpose and jointly agreed goals and values? | |
| **2** Does the team have a full complement of competencies? | |
| **3** Are all expectations and roles established? | |
| **4** Are all talents utilised and developed? | |
| **5** Do team members understand how their roles fit in to the plan? | |
| **6** Are task content and processes in place and according to plan? | |
| **7** Do team members meet, communicate, solve issues and make decisions | |
| **8** Do they celebrate differences, handle conflict and challenge each other? | |
| **9** Do they provide support for each other and give positive feedback? | |
| **10** Are there desired rewards aligned to mutual accountability? | |
| **11** Do they jointly set stretching goals and pursue opportunities? | |
| **12** Do they enjoy autonomy, responsibility and accountability? | |
| **13** Is a spirit of innovation maintained? | |
| **14** Are there good diplomatic relations and collaborations with others? | |

| |
| --- |
| If your total score is 20 or less, you do not really have a high performing team. If your answers score between 21 and 39 you have an average team. If your score totals 40 or more, you are well on the way to having a high-performance team. |

*There is no 'I' in team.*
Old saying

Source: with acknowledgement to Richard Livesey-Haworth

## Read around

*The art of captaincy*, M. Brearley

*The last word on power*, T. Goss

*Winning*, Sir Clive Woodward

## Links to other leadership tips

Leadership tip **86**

# Lead a dispersed or remote TEAM

*Leadership is practised
not so much in words
as in attitude and
actions.*

Harold Geneen,
former CEO, ITT

As globalisation increases and organisations become more complex it is increasingly unusual for senior leaders to be located in the same place as the majority of their people. Teams can be spread around the world and across many different specialisms. People working on projects can be from a wide variety of backgrounds and are not necessarily employees of the organisation. Indeed many teams nowadays exist only in virtual 'chat rooms' – brought together for a short time to serve a particular need.

Effective communication remains the key challenge of leading dispersed teams. It is the leader's responsibility to ensure that the entire team is enthused by the vision and understands the contribution the team and each individual makes to achieving it. The leader's overriding role is to develop good working relationships with those involved, build trust and keep two-way feedback flowing freely – essentially the same as for a team in the next office. When the team is dispersed it takes more time and effort and requires serious commitment from the outset.

→ Get out and about and meet people as much as possible – more often than you first think you can fit in. People need to see and speak to you before they will be willing to trust you. Concentrate on listening to their issues rather than talking about yours.

→ Speak to people regularly either in person or by phone and encourage them to write, phone and e-mail you and other team members as much as they need to. If necessary, establish mutual rules and guidelines as to when you and they can be disturbed.

→ Where it is not sensible to meet in person, use video links as much as possible, both for one-to-one discussions and for team meetings.

→ Encourage all team members to share information, keep everyone up to date with what is happening and meet often in small groups.

→ Have a rule that all new contacts should be made by (video) phone or in person, not by e-mail or post.

→ Hold team celebration meetings as often as possible – at least once a year – and make sure that you do not always have these nearest to your location.

→ Make all face-to-face team meetings as interesting, amusing and special as possible, hold them regularly and concentrate on team development issues as well as company and team briefings.

→ Respond actively and promptly to requests for help, be your team members' coach and help them to solve their own problems.

→ Use information systems that tell you how well, rather than what, they are doing.

→ Make all written and e-mail communications as personal as you can and remember family names, events, birthdays and other special occasions.

## In practice...

*Jim was appointed leader of a large team of specialists scattered across the British Isles. He quickly realised that some areas were more effective than others, there was very little cooperation between them and that battles about boundaries and influence were rife.*

*He spent the first six weeks after his appointment travelling to spend time with the people in every location. He made it clear that he wanted to meet everyone, not just the unit heads. He talked about the strategic direction of the organisation as a whole and his vision of how they could play a valuable role in it. He listened to grievances, objections and hopes for the future. Where straightforward issues were raised (such as equipment problems) he arranged for these to be dealt with fast. He undertook to come back to them about the rest at the end of his 'tour'.*

*Six weeks into the job, he had an all-day meeting with his senior management team (SMT). They reviewed everything he had learned, and agreed a plan of priorities for moving forward, including re-stating the standards and behaviours expected and tackling underperformance where that was an issue ... By the end of the day Jim and the SMT sent a joint e-mail to everyone in the team explaining what they could expect to see happening and when.*

*Jim and the SMT continued to visit the locations regularly to talk and listen to the people there. He told us that he wouldn't have believed how often he found that he had to repeat his vision so that people really began to believe in it. Nine months after appointment Jim told us that overall performance had improved, many of the 'difficult' people had moved on and that the whole team 'felt better'. He now found that he was getting suggestions instead of complaints.*

## Read around

*The art of captaincy*, M. Brearley

*Winning*, Sir Clive Woodward

*Greg Dyke, Inside Story*, Greg Dyke

## Links to other leadership tips

# Leadership tip **87**
## Deal with UNDERPERFORMANCE

In almost every organisation there are some people who are not performing up to agreed standards. Usually the rest of the team knows this and, unfortunately, sometimes so do other managers. As a leader you will lose the respect and trust of your team and your boss if you allow underperformance to continue, so you cannot afford to ignore it. On the other hand, enabling the person to achieve the standard will improve team morale and help deliver excellent performance all round – the team will see that you are not prepared to carry people.

As a leader your aim is to catch underperformance before it becomes an issue that requires the use of the disciplinary procedure. For underperformance to become a disciplinary matter could be regarded as a leadership failure. However there are situations when a leader inherits underperformance that has already, or should have become, a formal disciplinary matter. In these circumstances ensure that you have read and fully understand all the steps you need to take and the records you need to maintain, and do not delay invoking the procedure.

### Prepare carefully for the underperformance discussion

→ Be clear about the extent of the problem and whether you need to deal with it directly. Remember that if one of your managers has been avoiding dealing with underperformance in his team he is also underperforming, and it is his underperformance which you must handle directly.

→ Collect specific evidence of occasions and impacts that you can use as feedback. Include your own observation and knowledge as much as possible.

→ Consider whether there are any external factors such as ill-health or domestic difficulties that may need to be taken into account.

→ Remind yourself that underperformance is not the same as being 'no good'. The former is factual; the latter is a judgement about the person.

→ Decide what improvement is needed and what is likely to be achievable, and the time you are prepared to allow to see evidence of this.

*If a man is called to be street sweeper, he should sweep the streets as Michelangelo painted, or Beethoven composed music, or Shakespeare wrote poetry.*

Martin Luther King Jnr, civil rights champion

→ Be certain that you know your organisation's policy on handling underperformance and disciplinary procedures.

**The meeting**

→ Have the discussion in private in a work environment and preferably in the morning, early in the week, never on Friday.

→ Explain your concerns and give honest, factual feedback.

→ Listen to whatever explanations are offered and respond to requests for help, training or perhaps time off to deal with personal difficulties.

→ Be clear about the standard you expect.

→ Ask for suggestions about the personal goals that can be achieved in order to attain it.

→ Agree a SMART plan of action.

→ Keep the meeting short and businesslike. Avoid being drawn into personal criticism.

**Follow up**

Agree a date and time for review and stick to it. If performance has not improved agree the next steps with your boss or HR department.

### *In practice...*

*Many years ago when Margaret took on her first leadership job in a large office, the typists and secretaries took dictation and typed letters and documents using electric typewriters. The typing manager, Betty, was a formidable woman who was a real power in the office. Margaret soon found that the work she was getting from the typists contained a large number of errors and corrections (using correction fluid – Tippex) that resulted in retyping and delay. Margaret asked her boss and colleagues (all men) if they too had the same problems and discovered to her surprise that all were very dissatisfied but unwilling to raise the issue with Betty in case their work was delayed or affected as a result!*

*In the course of a week Margaret collected copies of all of the typing emerging from the pool and arranged to see Betty in her office on the following Tuesday morning. Betty was indignant but, faced with the evidence, eventually agreed that there were far too many errors and that these arose from lack of care by the typists, not poor dictation or handwriting, as they were not confined to certain individuals. Margaret asked Betty what she would like to do about the problem and, after a few moments' thought, Betty acknowledged that she had not been supervising the work. She had been taking the easy way out by being 'one of the girls'. She decided to re-arrange the allocations and oversee the output and monitor standards. She made it clear that she felt insulted that Margaret had raised this as an issue and wanted to know if everyone else felt the same way. Margaret was honest and said that while people were fed up with the errors they were too afraid of her to mention it! Betty laughed. Margaret said she had decided to do so because as the manager she wasn't happy with letters going out of the office full of mistakes and because she thought that Betty and the pool were capable of better. They agreed on a review in three weeks' time.*

*Within a day or two the errors had all but vanished. Thanks and praise began to flow into the typing pool and at the three-week review Betty arrived with plans for the induction and training of new typists, for a new post of deputy typing manager and suggestions for additional work which could be taken on thanks to the reduction in reworking. She also had a large bunch of flowers which she gave Margaret from all the girls in the pool, 'We were bloody angry with you but you did us a favour. That was the best thing that could have happened to us. Thank you'.*

## Read around

Your own organisation's disciplinary and grievance procedures

*Fierce Conversations*, Susan Scott

## Links to other leadership tips

**25** Embed new behaviours in line with the values in your organisation

**44** How to have a successful meeting with a difficult person

**84** Establish targets with individuals and teams

# Chapter 9
# Achieving extraordinary results as an organisational leader

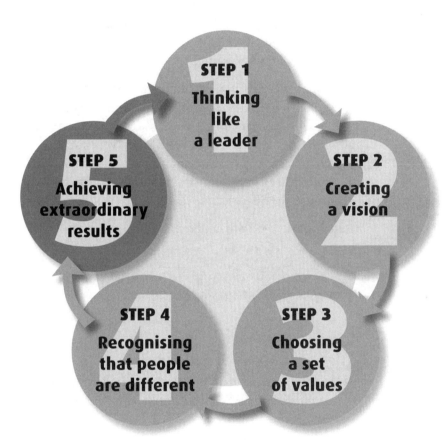

STEP 1
Thinking like a leader

STEP 2
Creating a vision

STEP 3
Choosing a set of values

STEP 4
Recognising that people are different

STEP 5
Achieving extraordinary results

# Leadership tip **88**

# Break a BLAME CULTURE

*The basic idea of 'Making it Happen' was that by getting rid of the crap, by freeing people to make their own decisions and to take their own risks, our programmes and services would improve.*

Greg Dyke, ex-Director General, BBC

Creating a blame culture is easy. All you have to do when something goes wrong is ask, 'Who did it? Whose fault is it?'. Before too long, you will find that getting to the bottom of whose fault it really is will become more difficult and mistakes begin to be more serious and harder to correct because they are discovered later. A blame culture is corrosive. It destroys trust, saps morale and energy, disrupts teams, and makes risk-taking and creativity impossible. Sooner or later, and it is usually sooner, it will ruin your organisation.

Creating or allowing a blame culture to continue is a serious failure of leadership. Breaking it requires urgent attention. Unfortunately doing so is neither easy nor quick but it can be done provided you as the leader are absolutely determined and relentless in your pursuit of different behaviour. You need to trust your people and earn their trust in return. Your personal example and that of your senior team will be under scrutiny all the time.

Recognise that you will need to encourage people to identify problems and mistakes. Be careful to deal with the facts and the impacts, not personalities and 'fault'.

There are some key steps you need to take:

→ At the outset say clearly that you have recognised a blame culture exists and that you do not find it useful or in line with your or the organisation's values.

→ Remind everyone that you want people to have ideas, take risks and be creative in their work, finding new and better ways for the organisation to flourish.

→ Treat all mistakes as real opportunities to learn. Ask, 'How can we delight the client now?' and 'How can we prevent the problem happening again?'.

→ Coach individuals to help them solve their own problems and increase their confidence and self-esteem.

→ Share the learning and celebrate ideas which have solved problems, e.g. improved internal processes or customer service.

→ Build the new standards of behaviour into all job appraisals and take action on backsliding.

At times during the process you may feel that you are trying to push water uphill – most leaders do now and then during this time. Don't give up. Keep leading by example and taking action to reinforce the different behaviours and one day you will realise that there is much more energy and enthusiasm around and that you have built a learning and supportive culture.

## *In practice...*

*Rachel was put in charge of a dispatch department in a busy whole-sale organisation. Sales were booming but dispatch was continually late, orders were often wrong and returns frequent. Rachel's job was to decide if the work should be outsourced.*

*Her initial meetings with the managers were frustrating as they all blamed everyone else for what was wrong, refusing to acknowl-edge their part in the problem. Rachel explained that the board had lost patience with the department, and that either they could work with her to turn the operation around or it would be outsourced. She said that she wasn't interested in who was to blame or why, only in what needed to be done.*

*At first progress was very slow. Tale-bearing was frequent and the majority of the staff appeared to be waiting to see what would happen instead of helping with the change. One manager in par-ticular, who had been with the organisation for a long time, per-sisted in 'having a quiet word' with her to point out the failings of his colleagues and make sure she knew of every small error. After several weeks of this Rachel invoked the disciplinary procedure and he left.*

*Within days the change began to be noticeable – people had more energy, made suggestions for changes that could be made and productivity improved. Dispatch became one of the most efficient departments of the organisation and Rachel was promoted.*

## *Read around*

*The art of possibility*, B. Zander

## *Links to other leadership tips*

# Leadership tip **89**
## CELEBRATE SUCCESS

We believe that all too often managers at work make too much of failure and too little of success. Lose a big contract and the team can be expected to be summoned into the boss's office for a dressing down and an evaluation of what went wrong. Win the big deal and it's off down to the pub to celebrate as a team. We think that most managers get this the wrong way round.

When you win the big contract is the time that the team should be summoned into the boss's office to evaluate what went right so that the success can be repeated next time. When you lose the big contract that is the time when you do not need to dwell on your mistakes. That is the time to head immediately down to the pub.

We believe that there should be compulsory evaluation of every success no matter how small. It is much easier to learn from success than it is from failure. We are not advocating that a celebratory event should not follow a success, only that the event should follow an evaluation of the success.

### *In practice...*

*Adrian led the team to win an order with a new major customer. The moment the order was confirmed, he summoned his team into the boardroom even though it was 5.30 in the evening.*

*He then set out his agenda. 'We are going to spend 30 minutes analysing what went right on this deal and why it went right. This is so that we can repeat this success next time we have a similar opportunity – and we have another in the pipeline in two weeks. Then I will take you all down to the Farmer's Arms to celebrate. Now Fran, can you take the notes and circulate them tomorrow?'.*

There are times when the team expects a celebratory event almost irrespective of the degree of success. There are other times when you can surprise your team with an unexpected celebratory event. It is about managing and exceeding the expectations of the team. When an event is expected, make sure that there is one. When there is no expectation – surprise them and exceed their expectations.

## Read around

*Fish!*, S. Lundin, H. Paul and J. Christensen

## Links to other leadership tips

# Leadership tip 90

# Manage CHANGE successfully

'Change management' was the mantra of the 1990s. There are dozens of models, books and conferences all peddling a preferred approach guaranteed to deliver success for your organisation. They are all based on a simple concept – that what worked in organisation A, with people X, at time 1 will obviously also work in organisation B, with people Y, at time 2.

A moment's thought reveals this concept for the nonsense it is. Organisations are all different: they are large, small, old, new, hierarchical, flat, entrepreneurial or established. Likewise, people are different and times change, so a universal model for managing change would need to account for countless starting variables. That is one of the two main reasons why around 80% of change initiatives are thought to fail. Others are that the initiative is a pet project of someone senior or that more attention is given to the bureaucracy of the change management programme than to doing things differently.

So, in a nutshell, there are **four myths in managing change...**

**1** Senior management knows what needs to change.

**2** Change management requires a major programme.

**3** Having a change management programme guarantees success.

**4** The absence of a change programme indicates a failing organisation.

**... and one truism**: the people in an organisation will make change happen when they believe in the goal, and their knowledge and suggestions are listened to and acted upon.

**Successful change**

This depends on the leaders being able to communicate real belief in the possibility of a better future and make it real for each group of listeners. To do that, leaders need:

→ real understanding of the business and the sector;

→ honest appraisal of the current reality;

→ courage to listen to the people in the organisation;

→ willingness to make tough decisions when necessary.

It is achieved as a result of clear focus on outcomes and great communication throughout the organisation.

From the **board and senior team**:

→ Initiating a new vision of the future possibility and being relentless about this belief.

→ Taking part and modelling the new behaviours all the time.

→ Being positive and open about the business reality and difficulties encountered, and being decisive about what is required.

→ Listening to staff – acting on 'quick wins', being available to discuss concerns, challenge negativity and underperformance and celebrate success.

From the **middle**:

→ Feeding info rmation back up the line.

→ Keeping the teams informed and involved.

→ Being positive about the potential gains.

→ Taking immediate action on straightforward good suggestions and dealing with underperformance and resistors.

→ Celebrating success.

From the **bottom**:

→ Joining in the discussions.

→ Giving feedback about the reality.

→ Making suggestions about how things can be done better.

→ Challenging one another.

From the **outside** (for instance, stakeholders):

→ Being positive about the ultimate gain.

→ Being patient and allowing time for the changes to happen.

→ Supporting the board and CEO.

Change is a natural part of the life of an organisation, not a 'bolt-on' or exceptional effort that will soon fade away or, worse, be replaced by the next initiative. Treat it as the normal way to a better organisation and better business and it will succeed. You will find that your people know what is needed. Your job is to find opportunities to ask, to listen to what they tell you and to have the courage and the wider knowledge to put it into practice.

### In practice...

*Greg Dyke, former director general of the BBC, describes one of his first successes there in his book 'Greg Dyke, Inside story'. 'When I arrived at the BBC I noticed that the open atrium in the middle [of the White City Building], was actually closed to the staff. It had been closed since the building was first opened and to go into the atrium you had to wear a hard hat.*

*I asked why the staff weren't allowed to use it and was told the magic words "Health and Safety". I asked for an explanation and some months later was told that staff couldn't use the atrium because there was no wheelchair ramp and it needed another exit to satisfy fire regulations. No one could explain why people had been wearing hard hats for a decade!*

*... I asked everyone around the table if they'd known all about this and why they hadn't done something about it. I remember the director of television saying, "We tried but it was too difficult so we just gave up". We all sympathised with this. We all knew changing things was hard.*

*So we ... arranged for the wheelchair ramp and fire exit to be installed and opened up the atrium. On the opening day I wrote a piece in* Ariel *in which I asked "How many equivalents are there around The BBC? Things which we can't do because someone, at some time, has told us it can't be done?".*

*I also held a party in the atrium that night for all the staff who worked in the building. As I wandered around many of them were excited and asked, "Does this mean we can go on the balconies now?" Or, "Does it mean my office doesn't have to be painted grey?". I found the man from property and told him about this. His answer was a classic, "Look at what you've started now!".'*

## Read around

*Greg Dyke, Inside story*, G. Dyke

## Links to other leadership tips

# Make the best use of CONSULTANTS

Consultants cannot take the place of effective management and leadership. All too often organisations call them in when the leaders want to duck part of their responsibility, from taking tough decisions about the size and range of the business to implementing a new health and safety policy. Even if you have called them in to help with a major business reorganisation, you as the leader must talk to your people, sit face to face with those you are making redundant and be prepared to live with the consequences.

Consultants can help when you have identified specific knowledge or skill that the organisation lacks and where that lack will only be significant for a fixed period. For example, you may need help in understanding a new raft of EU legislation or you may want specific expertise to help make your premises safe and accessible in the most cost-effective way. In those cases you would probably seek consultancy advice from the relevant experts. Or you might employ management consultants for a fixed period to introduce a new skill, such as performance coaching, to all managers. However, you would be foolish to hire management consultants to prop up a failing manager or take over running a change programme – those are leadership responsibilities you cannot shirk if you are to be successful.

Consultants are most effective when providing short-term learning for the organisation, on processes, procedures or management and leadership approaches, not by doing your job for you.

If you are thinking of employing consultants:

→ Identify clearly why you need external help with a project – this will usually be to provide expertise not available in the organisation e.g. on Six Sigma (a data-driven quality management system) processes training or outplacement counselling.

→ Identify the outcomes you want to achieve.

→ Consider and discuss how the relevant learning will take place. Ideally by the end of the project the consultants will have transferred knowledge and/or skills to your staff.

→ Agree a limited timescale for the project to run.

→ Identify and cost the internal people and resources that will be involved.

→ Agree fixed milestones for in-progress reports to you.

→ Be clear about and agree the potential risks and how these will be handled. In particular identify critical risks, those that will result in the project being terminated.

→ Agree the price – be careful of open-ended clauses which enable time costs to be rolled up and can increase the final bill dramatically.

→ Agree billing and accounting protocols.

## *In practice...*

The effect of using consultants ineffectively is summed up in this old joke.

A shepherd was with his flock one morning when a young man in a flash car stopped and asked the way. The shepherd told him and then the young man said, 'If I can tell you how many sheep you have in your flock can I choose one of them for myself?'.

The shepherd agreed, so the young man got out his laptop, hooked it up to his mobile and connected to a satellite, downloaded an image and an electronic count of the flock. He printed it out and handed it to the shepherd.

The shepherd agreed that it was correct so the young man chose an animal and started bundling it into the back of his car.

The shepherd stopped him and said 'If I can tell you what your job is, can I have my animal back?'. 'Sure' agreed the young man.

'You're a consultant', said the shepherd.

'That's amazing' said the young man, 'How did you know?'.

'You come here knowing nothing about my business and offer me information I already have for an exorbitant price. Now can I have my dog back?'.

## *Read around*

*Choosing and Using Consultants and Advisers*, H. Lewis

A few honest men are better than numbers.

Oliver Cromwell, politician, warrior

## *Links to other leadership tips*

# Understand, measure and change your business CULTURE

### What is a business culture?

A business culture is a collection of beliefs, values, priorities and behaviours that are generally accepted as the norm for a business group or organisation. It is the basis of the organisational personality. It is 'the way we do business round here' or 'the way we think about things' or 'the way we have always done our product innovation'.

Culture is fed and passed on through the stories people tell:

→ 'The time we stayed until midnight to get the order out.'

→ 'The day the storm blew the roof off onto the MD's car.'

→ 'The way they treated poor Jane.'

*Is he one of us
or is he a wet?*

Margaret Thatcher,
politician

So if you want to understand your business culture, listen out for the stories: at the office party, at the leaving drinks, by the coffee machine.

Individuals who demonstrate that they are in tune with the beliefs and behaviours of the organisation are usually accepted as a cooperative member of the team. They buy into the stories, accept 'the way we do things round here' and don't rock the boat too much.

Individuals who fail to demonstrate through their actions and behaviours that they are in tune with the culture are typically rejected by the team as 'not fitting in'.

A business culture is usually one of the last things to change and is probably the most important thing to change if you want to transform the way that things are done.

A business culture only changes if you:

→ recognise and accept what your business culture is now;

→ measure it objectively across all grades and types of job, teams, divisions and sites;

→ define what you want it to be and why;

→ take action to lead the change.

It is necessary to define explicitly the behaviours you want and the behaviours that you don't want. It is also necessary to present a compelling case for the need to change. This can be for survival reasons or for competitive reasons, but whatever the case, it must be seen as relevant by the staff.

For behaviours to change it is necessary to adjust organisational structures, processes, appraisal methods and reward structures in line with the new culture required. And the leaders must start to tell different stories:

→ 'Finance and marketing got together and came up with a fantastic idea for a new product.'

→ 'We've cut the delivery time by 20% without the team working overtime.'

→ 'You're expected to take risks around here.'

### How to measure a business culture

The exercise below will help you to find out how your organisation behaves in terms of the thinking styles described in Chapter 6.

If you complete the exercise yourself, the result will reveal your impression of your business culture. To get a reliable picture, you need to get people in the organisation or team to complete the questionnaires and then average the results. Plot the averages on the chart.

### Assessing your business culture

Have a look at the 32 statements below and, for each one, decide how true it is of your organisation. If it is:

→ very true, score 2;

→ partly true, score 1;

→ untrue, score 0

    **1** ♥ I can rely on colleagues to get the work done

    **2** ♥ Leaders keep their promises

    **3** ♛ We make decisions based on facts

    **4** ★ I know and am excited by our vision of the future

    **5** ➤ I have clear goals and targets which I helped to create

    **6** ♛ I am clear about my role and responsibilities

    **7** ➤ I take action within my responsibility

8 ♥ I keep others informed and consult widely

9 ≫ We deal effectively with those who underperform

10 ≫ I need to fire-fight to survive

11 ♥ We attract and retain first-class people

12 ♥ I am proud to work here

13 ★ My views count and I am listened to

14 ★ I know my leaders' views and I listen to them

15 ♛ I am kept informed of what is happening in the organisation

16 ♥ Teamwork is our preferred way of working

17 ♛ We are good at innovating but take care always to follow established guidelines

18 ♛ We make sure that decisions are fully supported by policies and procedures

19 ≫ We get things done quickly

20 ♛ We constantly benchmark our performance so we achieve best practices

21 ♥ I can trust the information I am given by everyone in the organisation

22 ≫ We deliver what our customers want

23 ≫ We deal with difficulties quickly

24 ♥ Reward structures are fair

25 ★ Reward structures support innovation

26 ≫ I achieve my bottom line

27 ★ I look out for how to improve delivery and for new ways of working

28 ♛ I am expected to report on everything all the time

29 ♛ We learn from mistakes so we do not repeat them

30 ★ There is always time to think

31 ★ We constantly scan the horizon for new opportunities

32 ★ We consider the impact of our decisions on all our stakeholders

Add up the score for each symbol and mark it on the diagonal axes on page 275. Join the four marks into a circle or a square as shown in the example overleaf.

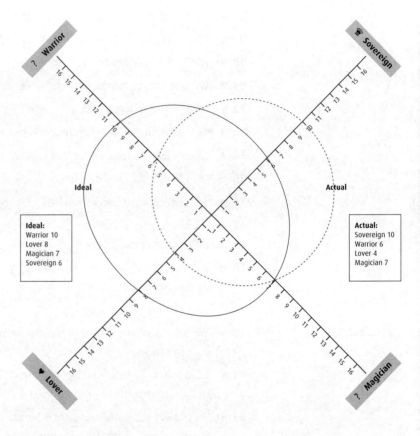

Ideal:
Warrior 10
Lover 8
Magician 7
Sovereign 6

Actual:
Sovereign 10
Warrior 6
Lover 4
Magician 7

Remind yourself of the behaviours associated with each of the thinking archetypes and see how these relate to your organisation at present. For example, looking at the completed chart above, this organisation will be careful and take care of its people. It may also be very slow at taking decisions, overly bureaucratic and resistant to change. Creative people may not last very long and tackling underperformance may be a slow and cumbersome process which does not achieve its aim.

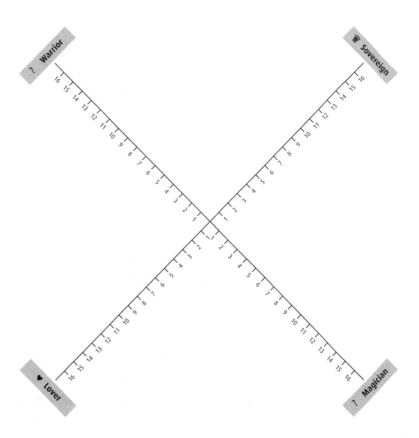

## Using the information to change your culture

First revisit your organisational values and decide how much each of the statements on the chart contributes to them, for instance if 'Leading by example' is one of your values then 'Leaders keep their promises' will be very important, so you would want that to score 2, and so on.

Then decide what behaviours are important to the organisation at present, for instance 'We attract and retain first class people' and 'We get things done quickly'. Give each a score of 2.

Remember that for each of the statements you are deciding what score you would ideally give if the culture really supported the change you know is needed. The importance of the scores set lies in the fact that each one recognises the relative contribution to the overall culture of the behaviour described. So the set of scores describes the desired state.

Add the results for each symbol and plot them on the same chart as before. The difference between the actual and 'ideal' culture will show you where movement is needed. (In the example the 'ideal culture' is shown by the dotted circle.) With the questionnaire results, you can then discuss with your team where specific changes need to be made.

The result of the survey will show you where the biggest differences are and enable you to focus your attention accordingly. Remember that people don't feel averages – they feel the differences between where they measure themselves to be compared with the cultural norms. The bigger the difference, the greater the discomfort.

## Read around

The rest of this book

## Links to other leadership tips

2   Identify what you want to change or how to spot what is wrong

16  Think creatively

23  Keep your promises

25  Embed new behaviours in line with the values in your organisation

27  Value the differences in people

28  Recognise the differences in people

29  Apply the universal model to leadership

30  Recognise and motivate a magician

31  Recognise and motivate a lover

32  Recognise and motivate a warrior

33  Recognise and motivate a sovereign

34  Use the universal model to evaluate your team, your key stakeholders or anyone else

88  Break a blame culture

95  Generate fun at work

Leadership tip **93**

# ENGAGE the whole audience

The people in any audience, or team, think differently. As a general rule each of them will, depending on their primary personality type, be most interested in the answer to one of the following questions: 'Why?', 'What?', 'How?', 'What if?'.

For any presentation to work, whether to a small team or a large audience, the presenter must cover all four aspects, whatever his or her personal interest. Failure to do so will result in some of the listeners switching off, getting the wrong message or remaining un-persuaded by the arguments presented. The consequence is likely to be confusion.

|  | Management | Leadership |
|---|---|---|
| **Directive – tell** | **What?**<br>➟ *Warrior* | **Why?**<br>♛ *Sovereign* |
| **Non-directive – ask** | **How?**<br>♥ *Lover* | **What if?**<br>★ *Magician* |

### Why?

Tell the audience why this idea, plan, change, initiative is a good idea. Link it directly to the vision of the organisation and explain both the outcome and the benefits you anticipate. Trust your people and tell them as much as possible, as early as you can, about what is proposed so that everyone feels involved. Make the 'why' real and relevant to the people in the audience. Talk about supporters to the fundraising team and about increased revenues to finance.

### What?

Tell them what needs to be achieved in order to deliver their part of the vision. Be clear about standards and timescales if these have been decided already. Where decisions are yet to be made, say so, be honest. Don't fudge issues or avoid giving bad news, you will only undermine your credibility.

### How?

Ask for the involvement of those closest to the task in deciding the detail of how it can best be done, recognising that achieving through others means respecting and engaging their expertise. *Listen* to the feedback. Ask how progress could be measured, how the right people could be found and for realistic timescales. Challenge the audience to go off and solve the problems. And then you must live up to that. Better by far to spell out the 'How' in detail if that is honestly what is required than to pretend to be consulting and listening and then to ignore what is proposed – you will lose their trust and undermine yourself.

### What if?

Ask for ideas, possibilities and views on risks. Outline those you have already identified and accept others. Don't justify – explain the bigger picture if needed. Do challenge them to think more widely and to imagine what could be if there were few restraints. And challenge negativity, get them to use their creativity to solve the puzzles they have identified. By listening to the answers to such questions and taking action on those that are appropriate, you gain the commitment of your people and will be trusted by them.

### *In practice...*

*Marian, a senior police officer, had a weekly catch-up meeting with her sergeants. She found the meetings tended to take a long time and get stuck in fine detail and she worried that some of the sergeants seemed to be leaving routine decisions to be discussed and decided by the group.*

*She decided to begin the next one by talking about the vision and values of the organisation, the aim of making society safer and of policing by consent. That led to a discussion of local priorities. Marian described it as the best meeting she had ever had, the sergeants really joined in the discussion, contributed their ideas for improvements and argued openly with one another before agreeing the way ahead. All left the room having enjoyed the discussion.*

## Read around

*Peak performance presentations,* R. Olivier and N. Janni

## Links to other leadership tips

# Leadership tip **94**
## **Run an ETHICAL organisation**

In today's consumer-driven business world, people are increasingly assertive in the exercise of their ethical preferences and are willing to back their beliefs by choosing where to spend their money. So it is in every organisation's self-interest to make the decision to organise its affairs along ethical and socially acceptable lines. The alternative may reduce costs in the short term, at the cost of longer-term sustainability.

Ethical organisations are those in which the organisational values accord with or exceed generally held moral norms, where these are explicit and known to all, the rules of operation are derived from them and systems exist to audit and report on compliance.

This framework of systems is known as corporate governance, the moral basis that underpins concern for social responsibility. The responsibility for the framework falls to the board and non-executive directors for plcs, to the boards of trustees in charities and voluntary sector organisations, and to ministers in respect of their departments of state.

Good corporate governance, and the behaviour driven by it, 'how we do business around here', provides an organisation with clear accountabilities at every level, from the board to the front line. Individuals know what is expected of them and what standards of behaviour are required. This leads to increased effectiveness and to a greater proportion of decisions being 'right'.

Corporate governance processes are only truly effective if they are based on shared understanding of, and belief in, the core values of the organisation and if leaders at all levels model these and challenge contrary suggestions.

The main principles of good governance applying to UK listed companies at present are:

→ There should be a clear division of responsibilities at the head of the organisation to ensure a balance of power and authority.

→ Levels of directors' remuneration should be sufficient to attract and retain the directors needed to run the organisation successfully, but no more so.

→ The annual report should contain a balanced and understandable assessment of the company's position and prospects.

→ Organisations should be ready to enter a dialogue with institutional shareholders based on the mutual understanding of objectives.

→ Formal and transparent arrangements must exist for an independent audit of the organisation's financial controls and reporting.

The rules of good governance force all organisations to do what the best have always done – deal honestly and transparently with their stakeholders, shareholders, customers and staff and report fairly on the outcome of all their transactions. And the leader's job is to champion that at all times.

## *In practice...*

*Responsible organisations are now going much further than the letter of the rules. They recognise five areas of corporate governance and social responsibility as inseparable.*

1 *To protect shareholders' investment, and to provide an acceptable return.*

2 *To win and maintain customers by developing and providing products which offer value in terms of price, quality, safety and environmental impact.*

3 *To respect the human rights of employees. To provide good and safe conditions of work and good and competitive terms of service. To promote the development and best use of human talent, equal opportunity of employment and the promotion of these principles.*

4 *To seek mutually beneficial relationships with contractors, suppliers and in joint ventures and to promote these principles in so doing.*

5 *To conduct business as responsible corporate members of society. To observe the laws of the countries in which we operate and to express support for fundamental human rights. To give proper regard to health, safety and the environment.*

### Read around

*Greg Dyke, Inside Story*, G. Dyke

### Links to other leadership tips

# Leadership tip 95
## GENERATE FUN at work

We spend most of our adult lives at work so we should expect to enjoy the time we spend there. As leaders we have a responsibility to 'lighten up' at least now and then and keep a sense of perspective about work as part of a wholly fulfilled life.

Developing a robust sense of the absurd and allowing yourself to laugh helps maintain a sense of proportion. Remember to take the job, but not yourself, seriously. Even a rueful grin can change your mood!

When we ask people if they enjoy working in the organisation the positive responses almost always include:

1   'I like the people – they are friendly and helpful.'
2   'We have a bit of a laugh.'
3   'The work is interesting and my contribution is valued.'
4   'I like my manager who is approachable.'

Much of this book is about how you, as a leader, can deliver 3. and 4. Yet it is 1. and 2. that make work fun.

In their book *Fish!*, Lundin *et al.* identify two key contributions to making work fun. The first is for people to remember how to play; the second is the willingness to make someone's day every day.

**Play**

This is how we understand our world and build many personal relationships. It can be team games, reading clubs, individual crafts or quiz night at the local. It allows us to be creative and take risks that too often become impossible once we don the business suit. To generate play at work think about how you could tackle tasks from an unexpected point of view. For example:

→   Use colours, posters, pictures, bright signs in the working areas and don't forget the floor – different-coloured floor zones for different activities, different coloured walkways leading to the tea and chill-out areas, the toilets, the lifts etc.

→   Use lots of plants to provide height, a sense of interest and individual spaces (and clean the air of computer-generated chemicals!). You might also consider an aquarium.

→ Provide tea and chill-out spaces with comfortable chairs, use coloured kettles, funky mugs and so on – they make people smile. Some years ago a large firm of accountants offered a prize to the employee for the best in-house mug design. A mock-up of a wine bottle label won. They are now prized possessions that always excite comment and the telling of the story.

→ Create an 'ideas zone' and provide lots of coloured pens, paper and craft materials. A senior civil service team once solved a difficult public policy issue while drawing rainbows and designing bags to hold them!

→ Always use lots of different coloured pens for writing on flip charts, use drawings instead of lists and find metaphors to help you sell your ideas – the approach will soon catch on and people will remember the 'tree of opportunities' better than the list of training options (even if they think it a bit naff!).

→ Use creative thinking techniques even in straightforward business meetings, e.g. make a storyboard of the budget forecasts!

→ Ensure that birthdays are remembered and marked – a few balloons and a card can make a big difference, while a card and a song will change the atmosphere dramatically.

→ Invite local holistic practitioners to visit the workplace once a month – staff will pay for the treatments, the professionals have a guaranteed client base, you give staff the half-hour for a massage or whatever and they return to work energised – everyone gains. Have one yourself too.

### Make someone's day

This is about being fully present for the other person, giving them your full attention and doing more than the bare minimum to solve their problem.

### Do:

→ Stop what you are doing, make eye contact and listen.

→ Ask what would help prevent the problem recurring.

→ Offer to mediate with other departments if that is appropriate.

→ Solve their problem with a smile.

→ Keep any promises.

**Don't:**

→ Keep dealing with e-mail or answer the phone while they are speaking.

→ Refer them elsewhere (take them if you really cannot help).

→ Say you'll get back to them 'later'.

→ Rush off before the issue has been resolved.

Source: adapted from Fish!, S. Lundin, H. Paul and J. Christensen

## In practice...

*Margaret once received a missive from head office exhorting all managers to follow the example of one office which had totally revolutionised its handling of post and telephone contacts. The improvements reported were indeed startling. Closer examination revealed that the office had been burned down so starting from scratch had been the only real alternative! This seemed rather a drastic approach.*

*Margaret shared the memo and her understanding with her managers and then challenged them to imagine what could be done differently if they too had to handle the aftermath of a widespread calamity. They used coloured tissue paper and balloons to indicate which sections had been affected each month. The 'game' quickly caught on, with some electing to be blue for flooding, some yellow for storm damage and others red for fire. Over six months the entire operation had been re-engineered by the people themselves and results were 20% better overall.*

*Moreover there was much more camaraderie and friendly chatter around the tea points, frequent jokes about burnt offerings, limp memos and so on, and the social club, long moribund, was revitalised and began running popular skittles evenings at one of the local pubs.*

### Read around

*Fish!*, S. Lundin, H. Paul and J. Christensen

*The art of possibility*, B. Zander

### Links to other leadership tips

# Distinguish between a business OPPORTUNITY and a business PROBLEM

*The first problem for all of us, men and women, is not to learn but to unlearn.*

Gloria Steinem, feminist, author

It is important to distinguish between problems and opportunities because it is human nature to deal immediately with a problem – 'that which is now' – even if its impact for pain is lower than the opportunity 'that may be next week'. We are used to dealing with priorities set by time, not necessarily by the gravity of a future situation.

The simple rule of thumb is that problems create current pain, opportunities, potential future pain.

For example we tend to deal with an urgent request from a senior manager for some internal information before handling a tricky supporter opportunity that has been around for a while. In our personal lives we tend to continue with a pleasurable habit whilst ignoring any longer-term damage that we know it will cause (e.g. smoking, drinking, overworking, or not balancing our lives well).

## Problems

A problem gives current pain and usually motivates short-term behaviour – we react to the pain by taking immediate action. At work this is usually known as 'fire-fighting' and is a high-energy pursuit. While it can be satisfying to feel a sense of achievement at having solved the problem it is also possible to get hooked on the adrenaline rush and to use fire-fighting as the normal way of working. This can have serious and long-term effects on both you as an individual and on the organisation you lead.

Continuous fire-fighting will eventually lead to increased physical wear and tear. You are putting your body into a state of stress that will take its toll sooner or later. While you may enjoy the buzz of fire-fighting, those around you may find it exhausting and de-motivating; always having to react quickly to today's crisis is not everyone's favourite working style.

Just as importantly, while you are dashing around putting out today's fire you are not taking time to think about tomorrow's conflagration or next week's potential disaster. You are in fact following, not leading; and your results, which may be fine in the short term, will probably not stand up to long-term scrutiny. Continual fire-fighting is the root cause of 'short-termism' and staff de-motivation.

### Opportunities

Failure to take an opportunity may give us pain in the future that we can only anticipate, so we always have a choice – ignore the opportunity in the hope that all will be well, or seize it and work to make the future better than the present. Recognising and seizing opportunities tends to motivate longer-term behaviours. You will need to plan and involve others, maintain your enthusiasm and interest and develop the team to be able to make the most of the opportunity. None of that happens overnight. You will not be able to rely on the adrenaline rush to keep yourself motivated so you will need to develop a sustainable vision and work on strategies to maintain and share it.

If you have been relying on adrenaline at work you may be tempted to seize every opportunity possible, with the same negative results. If you think you may be in danger of falling into that trap, find a critical friend or mentor with whom you can discuss the possibilities.

Use the tables in tips 97 and 98 to quantify problems and opportunities.

## In practice...

*Harry, a high-achieving civil service mandarin, was recognised as intelligent, well informed, creative and able to juggle many different issues at once. He enjoyed having a team of people around him and was energised by problems which he liked to solve quickly, even if that meant keeping the people for his next meeting waiting or working late into the evening. He dismissed suggestions that people might object to having to hang around for him and often said, 'Good people enjoy working with me, and I look after my own. If some people don't want to take the opportunity that's fine, they can go, that's their hard luck'.*

*Matters came to a head during a conference when Harry was, as usual, having side meetings and keeping several 'urgent issues' under control. He arrived very late for an important public presentation and the organisers, having heard from his office that he was running late, had filled in by asking the following speaker to speak early. When Harry began to speak he was unaware of the discussion that had gone before and as a result failed to pick up the mood of the audience. His presentation was not well received. He faced serious criticism from the floor and was not able to divert difficult questions. It was the first time his native charm and quick brain had not been enough to counterbalance lack of preparation and attention.*

*The experience taught him a painful lesson. He began to be a bit more selective about his personal involvement and to put time into his diary to ensure that he arrived on time for meetings.*

### Read around

*Managing at the speed of change,* D.R. Conner

### Links to other leadership tips

**35** Analyse problems

**97** Estimate the cost of failing to take a business opportunity

**98** Estimate the cost of failing to solve a business problem

**99** Think strategically

# Estimate the cost of failing to take a business OPPORTUNITY

### The cost of a missed opportunity

Consider each of the statements below in the context of an opportunity for your organisation. It could be investment in a research project, a new computer system, a change of distribution channel or a product diversification. Whatever the opportunity, highlight the one statement on the scale below that you think applies.

Now try to put an estimated value on failing to take this potential opportunity. For example, is this a missed opportunity which would cost £50 million, £500,000 or £50,000? This should be a guide to the amount of time and energy you put into the initiative.

**High cost**
**Most attention**

**Business imperative**

1   We will miss a key element in moving from a 'leader' to 'market dominance'.

2   We will miss a key element in moving from 'first class' to 'leader'.

3   We will miss a key element in moving from 'mid-stream' to 'first class'.

4   We will miss a powerful strategic advantage.

5   We will miss a significant strategic advantage.

6   We will miss a slight strategic advantage.

7   We will miss a powerful tactical advantage.

8   We will miss a significant tactical advantage.

9   We will miss a slight tactical advantage.

10  We will miss something pleasant and rewarding.

Source: with acknowledgment to D.R Conner, *Managing at the speed of change* and Richard Livesey-Haworth

**Low cost**
**Least attention**

**Good idea**

## In practice...

*In Brian's experience, when considering a potential acquisition, almost always the focus of the acquisition team is on the prospective price and the impact of merging two balance sheets and profit and loss accounts. In reality equal focus should be on an analysis of the cost of missing the opportunity.*

*With one potential acquisition the team decided that the business opportunity was at level 8 on the scale and that the potential cost of not going forward was in the region of £250,000. This conclusion was put to the board and the board decided not to proceed. As a result the organisation didn't waste a lot of senior time and effort in arriving at the right decision.*

## Read around

*Managing at the speed of change,* D.R. Conner

## Links to other leadership tips

**68** Take unpopular decisions

**96** Distinguish between a business opportunity and a business problem

**98** Estimate the cost of failing to solve a business problem

# Estimate the cost of failing to solve a business PROBLEM

*He who has a 'why' to live for can bear almost any 'how'.*

Friedrech Nietzsche, psychologist and philosopher

### The cost of an unsolved problem

Consider each of the statements below in the context of the problem in question. For example it could be a change in a supplier's business terms and conditions, a branch that is underperforming, a computer system that is causing delivery problems or a change initiative that is not working. Whatever the problem, highlight the one statement in the table below that you think applies.

Now estimate the cost of failing to deal with the problem. Is this a £50 million problem, a £500,000 problem or a £50,000 problem? The answer in the context of your turnover, assets or profits should give you an indication of how much time and effort to devote to solving it.

**High cost**
**Most attention**

**Business imperative**

1  Recovery will be impossible.

2  We will lose everything we consider important.

3  Recovery will be possible but unlikely.

4  We will lose most of what we consider important.

5  Recovery will be a long, expensive process.

6  We will lose something very valuable to us.

7  We will have to shift our entire way of operating.

8  The price will be terribly high.

9  The price will be more than we want to pay.

10  The price will be mild irritation.

Source: with acknowledgment to D.R. Conner, *Managing at the speed of change* and Richard Livesey-Haworth

**Low cost**
**Least attention**

**Good idea**

## In practice...

*Two functions within an NGO, marketing and publishing, were not cooperating as they should due to personality clashes.*

*One function tabled a complaint to the chief executive. On the evidence in front of him and without fully researching the extent of the breakdown, the CEO decided that the cost was between levels 9 and 10 on the scale opposite and would have no significant financial implications. As a result he decided not to intervene, suggesting merely that the two departmental heads resolve their differences between themselves.*

*In reality this dispute between two of his key departments meant that publicity materials about a major new publication range and the annual catalogue were not issued when expected.*

*With the benefit of hindsight, the chief executive ruefully admitted that this business problem should have been recognised as between levels 5 and 6 on the scale, with very significant financial implications. Had he carried out a rigorous analysis a major problem could have been averted.*

## Read around

*Managing at the speed of change,* D.R Conner

## Links to other leadership tips

**35** Analyse problems

**96** Distinguish between a business opportunity and a business problem

**97** Estimate the cost of failing to take a business opportunity

**99** Think strategically

# Think STRATEGICALLY

The purpose of thinking strategically is to helicopter above the detail in order to focus on the most critical issues for the future and to learn from the past. The aim of strategic thinking is to understand the business in the context of the outside world and to evaluate potential opportunities for the future.

In order to think strategically it is necessary to:

*Strategic planning, at best, is about posing questions, more than about attempting to answer them.*

Richard Pascale, business academic, author

1  **Challenge the status quo** by deeply examining the assumptions we are making about our business in relation to present and future spheres of operation. We need to ask what:

→ Is our Unique Selling Point?

→ Would be happening if we were delivering our vision every day?

→ Are we expecting to achieve in the longer term?

→ Will the sector/market/ UK plc be like in three to five years?

→ Would really delight our clients and stakeholders?

→ Is stopping us being more successful than at present?

2  **Put yourself in the shoes of each different internal and external stakeholder.** For example what would I think about this if I was the:

→ CEO of a major customer?

→ governor of the National Trust?

→ leader of a trade union?

→ minister in charge of a government department?

→ CEO of a competitor?

→ sales manager of your major supplier?

→ Etc., etc?

3  Only when you have done all that can you go on to ask **'What if?'** questions to encourage lateral thinking and speculate on possibilities. For example 'What if?' questions to release creativity include:

→ We had a magic wand?

→ We couldn't fail?

- → We had unlimited resources?
- → We had no competitors?
- → There were no risks?

And **'What else?'** questions to explore wider alternatives include:

- → What are other ways of tackling...?
- → What else might explain...?
- → What alternatives could be available...?

Remember not to fall into the trap of limiting your initial thinking with thoughts like 'We can't afford to...'; 'That's too risky.'; 'Bloggs would never agree to...'; 'That feels a bit frightening...'.

First let your imagination and creativity go as far as possible. You can take out the ideas that are too extreme at the second stage. Then, with a set of possible but challenging outcomes, you can begin to reality check them.

Ask yourself 'If we had actually achieved that what would be happening?'. And, once you have a fairly clear picture of what that possible future would actually be like, 'What's stopping us?'.

You will be surprised at how some things, which at first glance seemed impossible, become do-able in this way.

### In practice...

*John was appointed to a project team whose objective was to consider the possibility of acquiring another company. He quickly realised that the only way to decide whether this was a good idea was to think strategically.*

*The team needed to analyse the current balance sheet and profit and loss accounts of both companies and amalgamate them to get a first view. They also needed to think forward and predict what the joint balance sheet and profit and loss account could look like in five years' time. The team also had to consider factors beyond the numbers. These included market analyses, predictions of competitor reactions, alternative pricing models, the political and economic environment, technological advances, the development of a new business culture and the willingness of the two workforces to cooperate. They used 'what if' business modelling and scenario planning techniques extensively to test the best and worst case outcomes and risks. Only then could a reasoned evaluation be made.*

*This project taught John the skills of thinking strategically which he could then apply to all business problems and opportunities, not just when an acquisition was in prospect.*

### Read around

*The art of Japanese management*, R. Pascale

### Links to other leadership tips

# Leadership tip **100**
# Lead VOLUNTEERS

Leading a voluntary organisation requires all the leadership skills explained elsewhere in this book. But in addition it requires:

→ A passionate belief in the aims of the organisation.

→ Being at ease with and understanding the passion of others.

→ Schmoozing with donors whether you like them or not! Potential donors are everywhere. Be nice to everyone.

→ An ability to be an advocate for the organisation all the time – you are never 'off duty'.

→ Paying attention to the work environment – running a voluntary group does not mean you must use charity shop furniture or sub-standard equipment.

→ An ability and willingness to force through real business planning and process implementation. This is often difficult but it will ensure the survival of your organisation.

→ An ability to build effective working relationships with trustees – often committed amateurs with very different agendas and sometimes committed professionals who can really help you.

*Volunteering is not a soft option.*

Jeremy Oppenheim, former CEO, Jewish Care

## Leading volunteers

This depends entirely on your ability to make them feel valued, useful and to give them a sense of purpose and achievement. So it takes lots of time. You cannot just tell them what to do and be sure the task will be done – they can just walk away and there is no redress!

Key activities:

→ LISTEN, LISTEN, LISTEN, react; show you have listened and listen again.

→ Be passionate about the vision and return often to the 'better-world' outcomes you will achieve.

→ Say 'thank you' all the time and celebrate success.

→ Make working for your organisation as much fun as possible.

→ Build professionalism and skills – find what's in it for them and deliver as much of that as possible.

→ Give them real responsibility, avoid tokenism.

→ Keep in touch, constantly involve them in what is happening and listen to their views of where the organisation should go next.

→ Publicise what you are doing – everyone needs to be proud of the organisation, volunteers will 'sell' it for you.

→ Recognise that you do not have to accept sub-standard work from volunteers. Have a strategy for counselling sub-standard performers out of the organisation.

## In practice...

*Ann was appointed head of a day centre that cared for the elderly. The organisation was staffed completely by volunteers. She quickly realised that her job as leader of the centre involved making all volunteers, whether full or part-time, feel valued. Her task as leader literally involved 'walking the job' for many hours. She estimated that 70% of her time was devoted to this activity.*

*At the same time she adopted a businesslike approach to getting the work done and insisted that tasks were completed to a high standard, to budget and on time.*

*This worked. The volunteers all gave of their best, the day centre was written up as a centre of excellence in the national press and visited by the Prince of Wales.*

*The staff presented her with a cartoon of herself in action – busily walking from one department to another tapping her watch.*

## Read around

*Essential volunteer management,* S. McCurley and R. Lynch

## Links to other leadership tips

**12** Create a vision for your own operation

**24** Create a set of team or organisational values

**67** Develop and maintain trust

**71** Communicate openly

**82** Reduce resistance to your leadership initiative

# Leadership tip **101**

# Deal with the WITCHCRAFT that emanates from head office

Witchcraft is defined as any initiative coming out of a head office function that has been sold to the CEO as a quick fix to his or her problems. It is then imposed on a reluctant line management who do not believe in the proposed magic. They do know, however, that it is more than their career is worth to oppose this flavour of the month.

Witchcraft is extremely time consuming and never properly costed. It is rolled out worldwide without consideration for different cultures, states of organisational maturity or local managerial priorities. Witchcraft starts with a plausible theory that can stem from a guru such as the Harvard Business Review or from a management consultant. The theory however has no documented evidence that it will produce success. Where results are expected from it, the lack of them is never accepted as evidence that the theory was not soundly based. Examples can include the balanced score card, six sigma, ISO 9000, employee opinion surveys, communication audits, outsourcing and many more, when these are undertaken at senior management whim rather than in response to a real business need.

## In practice...

*Brian once worked for an insurance broker. Head office decided on the implementation of an appraisal scheme. Brian's part of the operation worked in very close self-managed teams that had superb internal communication systems. Brokers worked together on a day-to-day, hour-by-hour, minute-by-minute basis.*

*In these circumstances the imposition of a formal appraisal scheme which required an annual recorded meeting to monitor performance was irrelevant. This was witchcraft at its best. The new scheme did not add value to this part of the operation, it added cost, annoyed both managers and staff but had to be done to satisfy head office.*

When faced with witchcraft, ask the following questions:

→ What are quantifiable benefits that are expected from the witchcraft initiative?

→ What are the costs of implementing this initiative, including the real cost of the time of all employees involved?

→ What is the result of taking the benefits and subtracting the real costs?

If these three questions do not get you off the hook, proceed to the next stage. Ask, 'How does this help us to…:

→ …avoid high scrap rates on printed circuit boards?'

→ …provide a sensible structure for the indirect distribution channels?'

→ …or whatever your biggest problem is at the time.

Then state categorically that your own priority would be to deal with the biggest problem that you currently have on your desk. If head office really wants you to devote resources to this untried and untested initiative then the results of you doing this will be to neglect the biggest problem which will result in a financial loss to the organisation of £x million. Have your evidence for the figure ready and double checked.

If all of this fails then prepare yourself for the fact that you are just going to have to do it.

Source: with acknowledgement to Richard Livesey-Haworth

## Links to other leadership tips

**35** Analyse problems

**60** Break the rules and stay in line

**97** Estimate the cost of failing to take a business opportunity

**98** Estimate the cost of failing to solve a business problem

**99** Think strategically

# Appendix

# Applying the universal model to leadership – a perception and behaviour preference profile

This is an analysis of personal perception and behaviour responses to situations, time, space and people (or, finding where you sit in the model).

### Directions for use

**1** On pages 304 to 310 you will see a number of statements. Please read each statement and its four options for action.

**2** Rank each of the four options for action by writing one of the numbers below in the boxes provided to the right of the statements.

**3** Please use only the numbers 6, 3, 1 or 0 (i.e. no other numbers, such as 2, 5, 7) in this ranking process.

| Ranking number | Meaning |
|---|---|
| 6 | My most likely tendency |
| 3 | My second most likely tendency |
| 1 | My third most likely tendency |
| 0 | My least likely tendency |

Some questions will seem to refer to relaxed situations at home, with friends or on holiday. Others will seem to refer to more pressured situations at work. This survey should take approximately 30 minutes to complete, so please don't take too long to decide on each statement. When selecting your ranking scores please base your decisions on what you believe you would typically do in each situation, not on what you feel you ought to do or would like to be able to do.

**There are no right or wrong answers.** In your responses please be as honest with yourself as possible. This survey can be a powerful document if completed correctly. In doing so you will learn much about yourself and others.

**Example**

**When I have to tackle a problem at work, I tend or prefer to:**

| | |
|---|---|
| A. collect the information required and make a good plan (my 3rd choice) | 1 |
| B. take practical action as soon as possible (my 1st choice) | 6 |
| C. consider many different options and possibilities (my 4th choice) | 0 |
| D. obtain the views and involvement of others (my 2nd choice) | 3 |

The questionnaire should be completed in a quiet environment with no distractions.

**1 An enjoyable weekend for me is when I:**

| | |
|---|---|
| A. can be active, making things, doing things or spending time outdoors | |
| B. plan the activities so as not to waste time | |
| C. spend an enjoyable time with family and friends | |
| D. escape by reading novels or mind-expanding books | |

**2 Friends who know me well regard me as someone who is:**

| | |
|---|---|
| A. imaginative and intellectual, but perhaps too idealistic | |
| B. caring and helpful, but too emotional at times | |
| C. a logical and rational thinker, but on occasions too formal | |
| D. down to earth and to the point, but occasionally confrontational | |

**3 Going to the cinema or theatre I tend to prefer shows that:**

| | |
|---|---|
| A. exhibit historical accuracy, attention to detail and good research | |
| B. are realistic, action-based and have fast-moving story lines | |
| C. are original and somewhat deep, to open and enlighten my mind | |
| D. are based on the biographies or real lives of interesting people | |

**4 To improve the quality of work I believe that most of the time we need to:**

| | |
|---|---|
| A. take direct action on the most pressing concrete issue to save time | |
| B. seek to create a totally innovative work system | |
| C. discuss the problem with all colleagues to get their different views | |
| D. collect measurable data to quantify and analyse the problem | |

**5 Most disagreements at work are due to:**

| | |
|---|---|
| A. people who avoid or can't come to terms with a logical argument | |
| B. narrow-minded people incapable of seeing new ideas/approaches | |
| C. uncaring people who lack an understanding of the feelings of others | |
| D. individuals who lack the ability to take the practical action required | |

**6 If my team at work had to produce a plan I would encourage them to:**

| | |
|---|---|
| A. develop innovative strategies and seek novel or new approaches | |
| B. keep it short, useful and focused on practical 'key task' activities | |
| C. collect relevant data for analysis to ensure proven conclusions | |
| D. ensure everyone has a contributing role and input | |

**7 When discussing issues with friends, I like to:**

| | |
|---|---|
| A. get straight to the point and focus quickly on key items | |
| B. be certain of my facts and information before expressing a view | |
| C. show understanding and empathy by exchanging views and feelings | |
| D. explore hidden, unknown or unexplored issues | |

**8 I like my home environment to reflect my:**

| | |
|---|---|
| A. interests in new, original and innovative design concepts | |
| B. feelings of life, family and past memories | |
| C. sense of order, structure and good taste | |
| D. need for useful and practical work demands | |

**9 When buying something new like a television, car or gadget, I usually:**

| | |
|---|---|
| A. obtain quality specifications/performance data to know what I am buying | |
| B. look for practical and useful product features and buy at a keen price | |
| C. look for something distinctively different, novel or unique | |
| D. seek out the recommendations of friends and colleagues | |

**10 Under pressure, effective leadership is primarily about:**

| | |
|---|---|
| A. showing others the way from self-developed, real-world experiences | |
| B. being able to envision whole new business possibilities and horizons | |
| C. being able to touch people's hearts and create motivation in everyone | |
| D. having expertise, knowledge and proven administrative skills | |

**11  When working on a new task at work, I prefer my 'teacher' to:**

| | |
|---|---|
| A. | work through a written brief with all necessary steps, details and data |
| B. | explain to me how the task fits into the big picture |
| C. | use a patient, supportive and helpful approach to my efforts |
| D. | briefly show me how to do things and then let me do it myself |

**12  When dealing with difficult human situations it is best to:**

| | |
|---|---|
| A. | look for hidden issues to gain a wider perspective |
| B. | keep a focus on the task in hand and take decisive action |
| C. | keep the conversation rational and logical |
| D. | allow time for people to 'let off steam' and get things 'off their chests' |

**13  My most enjoyable holidays have usually included:**

| | |
|---|---|
| A. | a good deal of outdoors activity, like walking, sports, sailing etc. |
| B. | thorough advanced planning and organisation so that all goes well |
| C. | meeting and making new friends and enjoying their company |
| D. | visiting unusual or strange places to create new experiences |

**14  The people I relate to quickest and best are:**

| | |
|---|---|
| A. | highly imaginative and philosophical with creative thoughts and views |
| B. | warm, sincere and friendly; interested in others |
| C. | logical and rational thinkers |
| D. | practical in thought with a real-world experience in doing things |

**15  When I drive to a place of interest I will probably:**

| | |
|---|---|
| A. | consult a map and lay out a route before I start |
| B. | take the most direct route and get there in the shortest possible time |
| C. | select a lesser known route for change and variety |
| D. | obtain the best advice from others in the know |

**16 Often when faced with a conflict of work priorities, I try to:**

| | |
|---|---|
| A. take direct action on the most pressing issue to save time | |
| B. open up issues with exploratory questions to get the big picture | |
| C. deal with issues which are a concern to others or are needed by others | |
| D. proceed based on factual evidence and clear logical steps | |

**17 When faced with work pressures to get something done I usually:**

| | |
|---|---|
| A. analyse the job and plan a logical solution to the task | |
| B. try to envision the total job and find new approaches | |
| C. consult with colleagues to benefit from their helpfulness | |
| D. simply tackle things one at a time with direct actions | |

**18 Too often the failure of people to be effective at work is because they:**

| | |
|---|---|
| A. lack an appreciation of the importance of theories and concepts | |
| B. don't take decisions and action quickly enough | |
| C. don't understand the need for correct data and good procedures | |
| D. ignore the feelings and personal opinions of others | |

**19 To me 'real understanding' in communicating with others is achieved by:**

| | |
|---|---|
| A. talking about concrete issues with a genuine sense of practicality | |
| B. structured, step-by-step, logical and well-reasoned thinking | |
| C. showing genuine interest in the views and opinions of others | |
| D. creating new levels of awareness and mind-expanding concepts | |

**20 To my mind a successful day at home means:**

| | |
|---|---|
| A. seeing new possibilities come into existence | |
| B. meeting and communicating effectively with family and friends | |
| C. planning, prioritising and taking time to complete jobs well | |
| D. completing my most pressing tasks as soon as possible | |

**21 People who irritate me in conversation are those who:**

| | |
|---|---|
| A. present arguments without facts, information or proven evidence | |
| B. talk too much and fail to get to the point quickly | |
| C. usually have nothing new to say | |
| D. lack sincerity, warmth and genuine concern | |

**22 For business plans to be effective it is important that they:**

| | |
|---|---|
| A. are a brief document which is realistic and very practical | |
| B. take into account all future product and service options and possibilities | |
| C. take into account the contributions of all of the people at work | |
| D. are based on facts, are well thought through and financially costed | |

**23 In situations with tight deadlines I find it best to:**

| | |
|---|---|
| A. sort out and assess steps according to facts, data and priority | |
| B. explore novel approaches and seek innovative ideas | |
| C. obtain help by using the resources of the team | |
| D. take the lead with personal direct action on the tasks | |

**24 When pressured, effective business decisions must be based on:**

| | |
|---|---|
| A. an ability to see the whole picture of inter-related complexities | |
| B. reality-based experiences of actually having done things yourself | |
| C. objective facts, logical proof and reasoned alternatives | |
| D. a collective consensus of group-based opinions, feelings and views | |

**25 I am most relaxed when I am:**

| | |
|---|---|
| A. carrying out practical, physical jobs or tasks | |
| B. doing things that are part of planned achievement activities | |
| C. spending time with good friends or close companions | |
| D. doing things that lead to the discovery of new ideas and experiences | |

**26  I feel that I am best able to help friends with their problems by:**

| | |
|---|---|
| A. encouraging them to see new options and future possibilities | |
| B. showing understanding and getting them to talk through how they feel | |
| C. helping them to analyse their problems | |
| D. encouraging them to take action to deal with obvious difficulties | |

**27  Given plenty of time to do a job I prefer to:**

| | |
|---|---|
| A. gather accurate data and analyse probable alternatives | |
| B. look for physical and tangible signs of real problem areas | |
| C. stand back from the problem to visualise an overall approach | |
| D. consult others to discuss where efforts should be best applied | |

**28  I believe the most significant factor in improving work output is:**

| | |
|---|---|
| A. taking immediate action on problems as soon as they occur | |
| B. being able to find imaginative ways to alter or change methods | |
| C. practising true cooperation and working effectively with colleagues | |
| D. collecting measurable data to keep control over planned activities | |

**29  When pressured to make decisions in given situations I normally:**

| | |
|---|---|
| A. try to assess the probabilities of certain selected logical outcomes | |
| B. try to form a model or concept of projected future scenarios | |
| C. consider the impact my decision will have on the lives of others | |
| D. decide on what needs immediate attention and action | |

**30  In situations where I sense time pressures I tend to:**

| | |
|---|---|
| A. procrastinate as I seek fresh or imaginative approaches | |
| B. focus on immediate needs and then take action | |
| C. assess the data and proceed logically | |
| D. be careful and follow my past experiences as to what is important | |

## Plot your scores

To plot your score in both relaxed and pressurised situations, transfer the scores from the boxes on pages 304–309 to the labelled boxes in the left-hand table below. The numbers above each column relate to the questionnaire numbers above. Transfer the totals across to the relevant highlighted box on the right. Finally, add up the scores in the vertical columns and write the totals in the labelled boxes at the bottom of the right-hand table.

### Plotting your score – relaxed situations

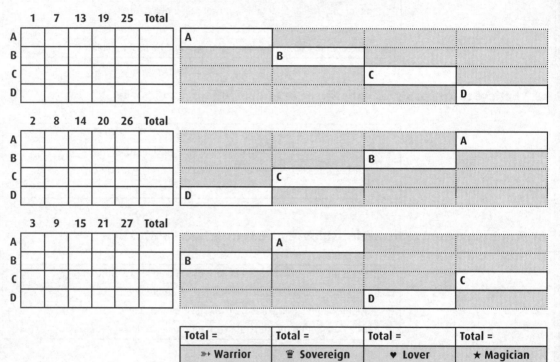

| Total = | Total = | Total = | Total = |
|---------|---------|---------|---------|
| ➵ Warrior | ♛ Sovereign | ♥ Lover | ★ Magician |

**Cumulative totals should be 150 points**

## Plotting your score – pressured situations

| | 4 | 10 | 16 | 22 | 28 | Total |
|---|---|---|---|---|---|---|
| A | | | | | | |
| B | | | | | | |
| C | | | | | | |
| D | | | | | | |

| | 5 | 11 | 17 | 23 | 29 | Total |
|---|---|---|---|---|---|---|
| A | | | | | | |
| B | | | | | | |
| C | | | | | | |
| D | | | | | | |

| | 6 | 12 | 18 | 24 | 30 | Total |
|---|---|---|---|---|---|---|
| A | | | | | | |
| B | | | | | | |
| C | | | | | | |
| D | | | | | | |

|  |  |  |  |
|---|---|---|---|
| A | | C | B |
| | D | | |
| | A | C | B |
| D | | | |
| | | | A |
| B | C | D | |
| Total = | Total = | Total = | Total = |
| ➵ Warrior | ♛ Sovereign | ♥ Lover | ★ Magician |

## Cumulative totals should be 150 points

You can use this process to identify your team members' styles and where you have overlaps and gaps. Plot the results on the chart on the next page.

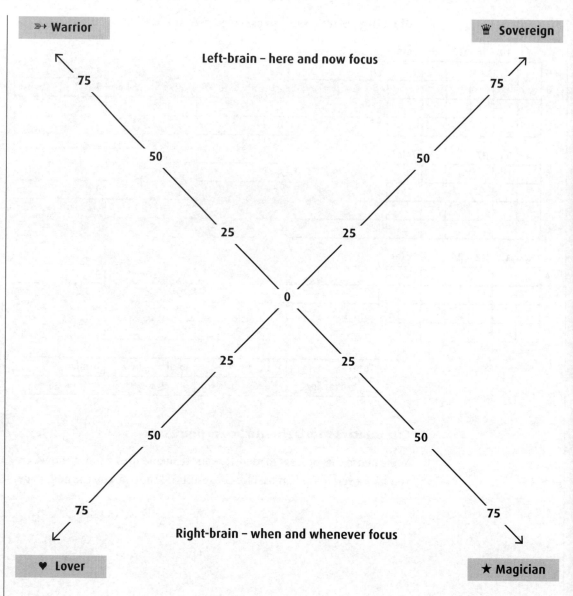

# References

Abse, J., *My LSE*, Robson Books, 1977

Adair, J., *The action centred leader*, The Industrial Society, 1988

Axelrod, A., *Elizabeth I CEO*, Prentice Hall Press, 2000

Back, K., and K., *Assertiveness at work*, McGraw-Hill, 1982

Barker, A., *Creativity for managers*, The Industrial Society, 1995

Belbin, M., *Management teams, why they succeed or fail*, Butterworth-Heinemann, 1981

Bennis, W. and Goldsmith, J., *Learning to lead*, Nicholas Brealey, 1997

Bennis, W. and Townsend, R., *Reinventing leadership*, Piatkus, 1995

Bennis, W., Spreitzer, G. and Cummings, T. eds, *The future of leadership*, Jossey-Bass Publishers, San Francisco, 2001

Bichenco, J., *Quality 75, towards six sigma performance in service and manufacturing*, Picsie, 2002

Blanchard K. and Johnson, S., *The one minute manager*, Harper Collins, 2004

Brearley, M., *The art of captaincy*, Coronet, 1988

Bridges, W., *Creating you & co.*, Nicholas Brealey, 1997

Butler, G. and Hope, T., *Managing your mind*, Oxford University Press 1995

Carnegie, D., *How to win friends and influence people*, Ebury Press, 1998

Chase, C., *The manager as a leader*, The Industrial Society, 1989

Clutterbuck, D., *Mentoring executives and directors*, Butterworth, 1999

Collins, J., *Good to great*, Harper Collins, 2001

Conner, D.R., *Managing at the speed of change*, Villard, 1993

Cook, L. and Rothwell, B., *The X & Y of leadership*, The Industrial Society, 2000

Covey, S., *The seven habits of highly effective people*, Simon and Schuster, 1992

Covey, S. and Merrill, A., *First things first*, Simon and Schuster, 1994

Csikszentmihalyi, M., *Flow, the psychology of happiness*, Rider, 1998

Daft, R., *Leadership theory and practice*, The Dryden Press, 1999

de Bono, E., *Lateral thinking*, Little, Brown & Company, 1985

de Bono, E., *Six thinking hats*, Little, Brown & Company 1985

Downey, M., *Effective coaching*, Orion Business Books, 1999

Dyke, G., *Greg Dyke, Inside story*, Harper Collins, 2004

Eckes, G., *Making six sigma last*, John Wiley and Sons, 2001

Edwards, B., *Drawing on the right side of the brain*, Fontana, 1982

Ellinor, L. and Gerrard, G., *Dialogue*, John Wiley & Sons, 1998

Fennell, M., *Overcoming low self-esteem*, Robinson, 1999

Fisher, R. and Ury, W., *Getting to yes*, Arrow, 1987

Fromm, E., *To have or to be*, Abacus, 1979

Fulton, R., *Common sense leadership*, Ten Speed Press, 1995

Gallwey, T., *The inner game of tennis*, Pan, 1986

Garnett, J., *The work challenge*, The Industrial Society, 1973

Gleick, J., *Chaos, the amazing science of the unpredictable*, Minerva, 1997

Goleman, D., *Emotional intelligence*, Bloomsbury, 1996

Goss, T., *The last word on power*, Bantam, 1995

Grout, J. and Perrin, S., *Kick start your career*, John Wiley & Sons, 2001

Giuliani, R., *Leadership*, Little, Brown & Company, 2002

Handy, C., *Waiting for the mountain to move*, Arrow, 1995

Handy, C., *The hungry spirit*, Hutchinson, 1997

Harris, T., *I'm OK, you're OK*, Arrow, 1995

Hartley, M., *The good stress guide*, Sheldon Press, 1995

Hersey, P. and Blanchard, K., *Management of organisational behaviour, utilising human resources*, Prentice Hall, 1988

Hill, G., *Masculine and feminine, the natural flows of opposites in the psyche*, Shambala, 1992

Jeffers, S., *Feel the fear and do it anyway*, Arrow, 1991

Johnson R. and Swindley, D., *Awaken your inner power*, Element, 1995

Katzenbach, J. and Smith, D., *The wisdom of teams*, McGraw-Hill, 1998

Kets de Vries, M., *The leadership mystique*, FT Prentice Hall, 2001

Kolb, D., *Experiential learning*, Prentice Hall, 1984

Kouzes, J. and Posner, B., *The leadership challenge*, Jossey-Bass, 1995

Kraus, D., *Sun-Tzu, The art of war for executives*, Nicholas Brealey, 1996

Kroeger, O. and Thuesen, J.M., *Type talk at work,* Tilden Press, 1992

Landsberg, M., *The Tao of coaching*, Harper Collins, 1996

Lawrence, G., *People types and tiger stripes*, Center for Applications of Psychological Type Inc., 1996

Lewis, H., *Choosing and Using Consultants and Advisers*, Kogan Page, 2006

Loeb, M. and Kindel, S., *Leadership for dummies*, IDG Books Worldwide Inc., 1999

Lundin, S., Paul, H. and Christensen, J., *Fish!,* Hodder & Stoughton, 2000

Mandela, N., *Long walk to freedom*, Little, Brown & Company, 1994

McCurley, S. and Lynch, R., *Essential volunteer management*, DSC Publications, 1998

McKenna, E., *When work doesn't work any more*, Simon and Schuster, 1997

Olivier, R., *Inspirational leadership*, The Industrial Society, 2001

Olivier, R. and Janni, N., *Peak performance presentations*, Spiro Press, 2004

Pascale, R., *The art of Japanese management*, Simon and Schuster, 1981

Peters, T., *Thriving on chaos*, Macmillan, 1987

Posen, D., *Always change a losing game*, Key Porter Books, 1994

Pratchett, T., *The colour of magic*, Corgi, 1987

Rickards, T. and Moger, M., *Handbook for creative team leaders*, Gower, 1999

Scott, S., *Fierce conversations*, Piatkus, 2002

Shackleton, E., *South, the endurance expedition*, Penguin, 1999

Stettner, M., *Skills for new managers*, McGraw-Hill, 2000

Tice, L., *New age thinking for achieving your potential*, Pacific Institute, 1980

Wheatley, M., *Leadership and the new sciences*, Berrett-Koehler, 1996

Wheatley, M. and Kellner-Rogers, M., *A simpler way*, Berrett-Koehler, 1996.

White, Admiral Sir P., *Preparing for the top*, The Industrial Society, 1981

Whitmore, J., *Coaching for performance*, Nicholas Brealey, 1996

Whitmyer, C. ed., *Mindfulness and meaningful work*, Parallax Press, 1994

Williams, M., *Mastering leadership*, Thorogood, 1998

Woodward, Sir C., *Winning*, Hodder & Stoughton, 2004

Zander, B., *The art of possibility*, Penguin, 200